You Can Keep Them If You Care

Helping New Members Stay On Board

James A. Cress

Ministerial Association Resource Center
General Conference of Seventh-day Adventists
Silver Spring, MD 20904

Published by
The Ministerial Association
General Conference of Seventh-day Adventists

Copyright © 2000
General Conference Ministerial Association Resource Center
(301) 680-6508
Printed in Canada
by Maracle Press
Oshawa, Ontario

Table of Contents

Introduction

This book presents an innovative and comprehensive plan for assimilating new members into the church. Based on the New Testament understanding of the church, it offers practical suggestions that can be used in most Adventist churches. The original study, done as part of my doctoral work at Fuller Theological Seminary, referenced the Seventh-day Adventist congregation at Marietta, Georgia, where my wife, Sharon, and I were privileged to pastor together.

Marietta, fifteen miles northwest of downtown Atlanta, is the cultural and governmental center of Cobb County, Georgia, one of the fastest growing counties in the United States. Marietta is also the premier suburban community of metropolitan Atlanta. Cobb County's population is larger than several states in the United States. Its public utilities, roads, schools, and hospitals, as well as other support structures, are undergoing serious restructuring as this community takes its place as a significant leader in the whole urban structure of greater Atlanta.

Churches of various denominations are responding to the rapid growth of Cobb County. I personally know of a dozen newly-planted congregations that have sprung up in recent years, including two new Adventist congregations as well as another three Adventist congregations that are in adjoining counties within twenty minutes' driving time.

The Marietta Seventh-day Adventist church is relatively young, founded in 1955 for the specific purpose of establishing Adventist education for Cobb County Adventists who no longer wished to transport their children to Atlanta.

Following a peak in the early 1980s with about 500 members and 300 in attendance, our congregation entered a phase of gradual decline. In 1989 the congregation was seriously divided on a variety of issues and average attendance dipped below 200. Then the church experienced an extended interim period between pastors.

Significant growth occurred between 1990 and 1997, with a current membership of about 900 and active attendance of 600-700. This rapid growth severely strained our facilities as well as our capabilities for adequately nurturing newcomers. Our challenge in Marietta was not recruiting new members—transfer and aggressive evangelism resulted in a steady influx of new members—but assimilating and nurturing them into the life of the congregation and providing them meaningful opportunities for personal ministry.

Much like the biblical description of the sowers overtaking those who harvest, we implemented these essential plans even as they were being developed. In fact, some of our attempts at improving the assimilation of our new members were already underway even as we designed our strategy.

Definitions

Whenever a topic is explored, particularly in a theological framework, it is essential to define some terms as they will be used. Otherwise, assumptions might be made by the author or conclusions drawn by the reader which would communicate something other than the intended meaning. Hence, I am providing a selected list of words and the definitions which underscore their usage in this book.

Accession: To add a member to the membership rolls of the Seventh-day Adventist church by baptism, profession of faith, or transfer. *Fifty members were accessioned into our congregation last year.*

Active membership: Members who attend church services on a regular recurring basis and reflect a lifestyle in consonance with the church. See "churched" below. *Our active membership is smaller than our book (official) membership.*

Adventist: Short form of "Seventh-day Adventist." See below.

Apostasy: Abandonment of Christian doctrines or lifestyle. Apostasy may, but does not always, lead to the member's being "disfellowshipped." If a church chooses not to discipline the individual in apostasy, they will likely refer to him/her as a "dropout." *Joe simply dropped out—we haven't seen him at all.*

Assimilate: To incorporate and disciple new believers and/or newly-transferred members into the life of the congregation and ultimately to employ their spiritual gifts in ministry. *We are developing a plan to better assimilate our new members into the life of our congregation.*

Assimilation process: This phrase includes the whole process by which an individual in North America moves through the various phases of the Engel Scale[1] from initial knowledge of Christianity through personal application and acceptance toward mature discipleship and personal ministry within the body of Christ. *However, in this book, the term is limited to those portions of the process that describe the incorporation of new members into the life of the local congregation.* As a point of reference, this would relate to items 0 through +5, etc., on the Engel Scale.

Baptism: The event which marks the new believer's entrance into the church—the church as both the body of Christ and the local congregation. Some denominations might refer to this event as *regeneration,* the *decision for Christ,* or *confirmation.* While Adventists recognize general decisions for Christ, such choices are measured within our denomination only as they are expressed in baptisms or professions of faith. This measurement system, which emphasizes the point in time in which converts are accessioned, often leads to accusations that evangelists play a "numbers game" with little regard to stabilization or assimilation of new members. *Thirty decisions for Christ were made and fourteen individuals experienced baptism.*

Caring church concept: A term sometimes used by Adventists in North America to place emphasis on the role of the local congregation to nurture the spiritual life of the members and to equip them for ministry within the realm of their personal spiritual gifts. *The caring church concept is not a program but rather a way of life.*

Casually churched: An individual who claims Christianity culturally and who may even hold membership in a local congregation but whose attendance is limited to special occasions or unique events and whose participation or financial support is minimal to nonexistent. *Of course I'm a Christian; after all, I'm an American.*

Churched: A Christian who is actively involved in the life of a local congregation by attendance, financial support, and participation in ministry. *Of course I'm a Christian. Jesus is my Lord and Saviour. Here is where I fellowship with other believers!*

Disfellowship: The removal of a member from church membership for disciplinary reason—the most stringent form of church discipline applied in Adventist churches. Disfellowshipment is usually preceded by censure, a lighter form of discipline which involves forfeiting church offices and privileges. Disfellowshipping is more often occasioned by ethical/moral issues rather than by doctrinal. *When he divorced his wife, John was disciplined by censure, but when he remarried another woman, he was disfellowshipped.*

Dropout: Interchangeable with *inactive,* the term usually connotes that the individual has made a conscious choice to leave, and the congregation has given up hope of reclaiming the individual to active membership. *Joe used to be inactive, but now he is a dropout!*

Evangelism: "To evangelize is so to present Christ Jesus in the power of the Holy Spirit, that men and women shall come to put their trust in God through Him, to accept Him as their Saviour, and serve Him as their King in the fellowship of His Church." [2] *This definition views evangelism as process more than event.*

Inactive: An individual who once was churched but who has voluntarily chosen, for whatever reason, to cease participation in congregational activities. Some inactive Adventists may continue financial support or lifestyle adherence even after ceasing attendance. This cessation of participation may have been occasioned by apathy, but more often it is the result of pain, whether real or imagined. *Of course I'm a Christian, but I can worship alone just as well as in a group.*

New member: A recently accessioned member who is within the first months of church fellowship. *John was baptized four months ago. We are happy for new members like him!*

New member stabilization process: The process by which the new believer is settled into the corporate experience of the church, both in participation and in distinctive Adventist lifestyle. Essentially the same as *assimilate* but with special emphasis on needs of new converts rather than new transfers. *It is important to keep new converts in a stabilization process until they are strongly rooted in their Christian walk.*

Non-member: Any individual who is not a member of the Adventist church. This term, which appears pejorative and judgmental, is likely used without any attempt at determining whether the person referenced is churched in another denomination or unchurched. *We had twenty non-member guests at last week's worship service.*

Profession of faith (POF): A term that describes how a person may enter membership other than by baptism. Since Adventists affirm baptism by immersion, this term is reserved for those who have been baptized by immersion in another denomination and now choose to join the Adventist church by professing their faith, thus indicating they have accepted the Adventist beliefs and lifestyle. *Twelve new members were baptized and five joined by POF.*

Seventh-day Adventist: An evangelical Christian denomination of about ten million adult members worldwide (about twenty-five million people consider themselves Adventists) whose corporate expression of faith is experienced within local congregations of believers and whose most notable theological features include worship on Saturday, the "seventh day," and their hope in the imminent "advent" of Jesus Christ. Adventists are well known for their emphasis on healthful living, charitable works of famine and disaster relief, global mission work, medical and educational facilities, high per capita giving, and activism in areas of temperance, religious freedom, and evangelism.

By the 1980s, the Adventist denomination was growing slowly in the United States, about 2 to 3 percent annually. Over 76 percent of Adventists lived in developing countries, whereas North America had only 16 percent, Europe 6 percent, and Australia/New Zealand, 1 percent. The great numbers of members added have shifted decision-making power bases away from the continent where the church was born, not without dramatic consequences for the denomination. For example, although 80% of the membership resides outside of North America, the denomination is still dependent upon North American members for nearly 80% of its global finances. Other consequences also impact the church. Gary Land says, "This shift held tremendous potential for changing the world demographics of the denomination from an older to a younger church; from a tradition-clergy-oriented denomination to a dynamic, lay-centered missionary movement; from a 'second generation' church to a first generation church." [3] This, indeed, is occurring in other parts of the globe, but it is not so in North America, Europe, or Australia/New Zealand.

Adventists believe they have a prophetic mission to proclaim an apocalyptic message to a judgment-bound planet. They emphasize obedience to the Ten-commandment law as a fruit/result of salvation. This emphasis has led some to conclude that Adventists believe in salvation by "grace plus works." This is not so. They, like other evangelical Christians, clearly affirm their belief in the good news of salvation by grace alone through faith in the shed blood of Jesus Christ.

The propensity for Adventists to value scholarship and to argue theology has led some observers, within and without the denomination, to wonder if abstract issues are more valued than people. Adventists in North America are attempting to rectify both this perception and this experience through an emphasis on the local congregation as a "caring church."

Transfer: A new member to a local congregation whose membership has come from another congregation of the same denomination by letter. Transfer growth is highly desired because it typically brings active, involved, and financially supportive new members into the congregation. *"We had several baptisms and professions of faith plus ten transfers!"*

Unchurched: An individual who does not participate in the spiritual life of any congregation except by rare attendance at sociologically occasioned events such as weddings, funerals, etc. *"Of course I'm an American and religion is a real part of our society."*

∼ Part I ∼
Conversion is a Process, Not an Event

Assimilating new members into active participation in the life and experience of any congregation is a challenge. When existent members of that congregation anticipate from new members a more radical lifestyle transformation than the new member may be capable of displaying, both the new members and the existent members are set up for disappointment, frustration, and, far too often, a seemingly inevitable parting of the ways.

While this is, no doubt, a problem for any body of believers, it has become particularly acute for the Seventh-day Adventist church in North America during the past 20 years.

Although the Adventist church is one of the fastest growing denominations worldwide and still shows a North American growth factor, albeit slowed, we must now grapple with the fact that for every three individuals who join our church, one member chooses to leave. While many of these individuals have been members for a number of years, far too often this exodus from fellowship is made by new members who have never been fully incorporated into the life of their local congregation.

As Peter Wagner so aptly states to his church growth classes, "Any scheme which separates evangelism and follow-up has built into itself the cause of its own failure." [4] The Adventist church has generally failed to understand the difference between the event of accession into the membership roll of the church and the process of assimilation into the body of believers.

I will attempt to demonstrate that any failure to view conversion as an entire process which includes awareness and investigation, instruction and indoctrination, decision and baptism, and, perhaps most importantly, assimilation and discipleship, is a failure both to understand our Lord's own teaching and example, and to experience in practice what we believe in theory—that the goal of the great commission is to make disciples.

While the emphasis of this book centers on the specifics of incorporating new believers (primarily) and new transfers (secondarily) into the life of a specific congregation—the assimilation/discipleship phase—it must be set within the context of conversion as a process leading to discipleship rather than conversion as an event leading to membership.

~

> "Any scheme which separates evangelism and follow-up has built into itself the cause of its own failure."

~

This issue of "process" versus "event" is a biblical concept that must become the driving factor in our theology of new member assimilation as well as a determining factor in those plans and programs which we implement in our attempt to assimilate new members.

Therefore, the purpose of Part I is to develop three theological imperatives for adequate assimilation of new members into the congregation within this context.

Chapter 1. Developing Disciples. A study of Jesus' gospel commission (Matt. 28) that challenges the all-too-typical Adventist approach to measuring evangelistic success on the basis of accessions rather than disciple making.

Chapter 2. Nurturing Newborns. A study of Jesus' own understanding of the status of new believers (John 3) which challenges the all-too-typical Adventist desire for new believers to experience sanctification concurrent with, or prior to, justification.

Chapter 3. Conserving the Catch. A study of Jesus' parable of the net (Matt. 13) that challenges the all-too-typical Adventist rejection of new believers who do not immediately measure up to expectations.

Chapter 1

Developing Disciples

Go therefore and make disciples of all the nations, baptizing them in the name of the Father and of the Son and of the Holy Spirit, teaching them to observe all things whatever I have commanded you; and behold, I am with you always, even to the end of the age. Amen (Matt. 28:19-20, NKJV).

The focus of Jesus' mission was to provide for the sins of a dying, lost world. He came to seek and to save the lost (Luke 19:10). He came that men and women might believe in Him (John 3:16). How did He accomplish this? What was His method? Christ's method was calling and building disciples. Humans were His method.[5] The Greek word for "disciple" is *matheteuo*, meaning a follower, a learner. The disciples were followers of Jesus and learners from Him. The great commission called them to do what He had done. They were to make disciples. This is the primary emphasis of Matthew 28:19. *Making disciples* is the main verb of the verse. The other verbs–*going, baptizing, teaching*–are subordinate.[6]

What does it mean to "make a disciple?" Obviously it means something more than mental acknowledgment of God's supremacy or even mere acceptance of Jesus Christ. Donald McGavran, the leading expositor of church growth principles, links discipleship inseparably with responsible church membership. Not until the new believer is linked to the body of Christ, formed into fellowship with other believers, and responsibly ministering for others have we made a disciple. McGavran says, "After nearly two hundred years of modern missions only a few out of the myriad peoples of the world have been incorporated in the church, i.e., been discipled."[7]

McGavran pioneered the concept of "disciple" as a verb. In his 1955 *The Bridges of God*, he began using "disciple" as a verb meaning "to help a people (a segment of non-Christian society) turn from non-Christian faith to Christ." Since that time he has refined the definition to include distinct phases of discipling:

D1 The turning of a non-Christian society for the first time to Christ.

D2 The turning of any individual from non-faith to faith in Christ and his/her incorporation in a church.

D3 Teaching an existing Christian as much of the truths of the Bible as possible.

McGavran's definition is excellent in two ways. First, it addresses discipleship as an action—an activity—of the church. Secondly, it shows that there is a process in stages of acceptance of Jesus Christ.

By the description of D1, however, we would find not many opportunities for this level of discipleship in North America. McGavran describes D1 "like an illiterate village in Zaire [Republic of Congo] which has resolved to build a school and send all of its children to school." [8]

Therefore, we will focus here more on D2 and D3, particularly that point at which the new believer is incorporated into the church and from there *discipled* (verb) into becoming a *disciple* (noun). To describe this process (D2 through D3), Allen Hadidian, pastor of Heights Evangelical Free Church, La Habra, California, offers a most helpful definition:

"Discipling others is the process by which a Christian with a life worth emulating commits himself for an extended period of time to a few individuals who have been won to Christ, the purpose being to aid and guide their growth to maturity and equip them to reproduce themselves in a third spiritual generation." [9]

In fact, Hadidian affirms McGavran's D-1, D-2, D-3 approach by identifying three phases of discipleship that correspond in meaning, although terminology might be different. Also, Hadidian's application might be aimed more toward North American culture, whereas McGavran's has a wider, global focus. Hadidian describes these three phases as Evangelizing, Edifying, and Equipping and identifies seven marks of a discipler's ministry: Guardianship, Example, Direction, Time, Commitment of One's Life, Numerical Limitation, and Friendship. An alignment of his definition of discipleship along with the three phases and seven identifying marks might be diagramed as follows:

[Friendship]	Discipling others is the process
	by which a Christian with a
Example	life worth emulating
Commitment	commits himself
Time	for an extended period of time
Numerical Limitation	to a few individuals who have been
Phase I	won to Christ,
Direction	the purpose being to
Guardianship	aid and guide their
Phase II	growth to maturity and equip them to
Phase III	reproduce themselves in a third spiritual generation. [10]

Value of making disciples

Thus the goal of the gospel commission is to continue the work that Jesus began by following the same strategy. Make disciples! Teach them! Enable them to reproduce their lives and faith in the lives of others for whom they labor. The ministry of discipling has value to the disciple, to the discipler, to the church, and to the world. For the new believers, values of discipling are many. Their rate of spiritual growth is increased. Their wrong behavior patterns can be arrested and stopped. They are better protected from the enemy. They are provided a personal friend who emulates Jesus' friendship to them. And they are provided with spiritual counsel.

> Continue the work that Jesus began by following His strategy.

The value of discipling for disciplers is that it brings joy to them (3 John 1:4; 1 Thess. 2:19-20). It purifies their lives. It develops their ministerial skills, and it provides an outlet for the knowledge that they have gained.

The value of discipling for the church is that it strengthens the body, develops godly leaders, and perpetuates God's mission to the world.

The value of discipling to the world is that individual lives are changed—lives of individuals who will inhabit Christ's kingdom! [11]

Seventh-day Adventists have historically accepted the goal of the great commission as being to so proclaim Jesus Christ as God and Saviour that men and women will place their trust in Him through faith and become responsible members of His church. However, for an ethically oriented, behavior-measuring group of conservative Christians, the "responsible" portion of this definition has sometimes been lacking in the lives of new members at the precise moment that existent members feel it should be most evident. Notwithstanding that the fruits of the Spirit are sometimes unobservable in the lives of "older members," we have been too quick to assign blame for this lack in the lifestyles of new members. We blame it on either insufficient consecration on the part of the baptized or insufficient preparation on the part of the pastor or evangelist.

Much of this problem grows out of a misperception of baptism (which for Adventists occurs simultaneously with entrance into the church) as a culminating, graduation-type event in response to appropriate doctrinal instruction, rather than understanding it as either the beginning of the Christian's life in Christ or even as another step in an ongoing process. We wish new believers would walk the Christian walk simultaneously with acceptance of Jesus Christ and being baptized. This problem, regarding new member assimilation for Seventh-day Adventists, is aptly stated and the solution ably suggested by Win Arn's discussion of a subtle, but fundamental distinction between evangelism and disciple making:

"Evangelism: Success is achieved when a verbal response is given by the non-Christian which indicates his/her personal endorsement of a new set of convictions reflective of the Christian faith. A "decision" centers around a point in time.

"Disciple Making: Success is achieved when a change is observed in the behavior of an individual which indicates his/her personal integration of a new set of convictions reflective of the Christian faith. A "disciple" centers around an ongoing life style.

"But because the goals are different, the *process* employed in achieving each goal is different." [12]

Peter Wagner calls this difference between those who make decisions and those who ultimately become responsible church members the "Follow-up Gap." [13] The product of evangelism must be disciples, not decisions. Failure to recognize this is a failure to fulfill the great commission through which Jesus sent His disciples into all the world to make disciples of all people, teaching them to observe all things that He had commanded.

Waldron Scott presents a balanced and interdependent relationship between evangelism for decisions and evangelism for discipleship, which he calls *discipleship evangelism*. He advances three theses:

"1. Discipleship is the true and ultimate objective of biblical evangelism.

"2. Qualitatively, evangelism is shaped—both as to content and style—by one's concept of discipleship.

"3. Quantitatively, biblical discipleship multiplies the fruit of evangelism." [14]

Being a Christian and being a disciple

It is imperative that the church understands that God's objective has not changed. God still sees that the world must be won to more than mental assent or an acceptance of "cheap grace" salvation. The issues are cosmic and eternal. Walter Henrichsen says, "Being a disciple begins with a proper relationship to Jesus Christ and having on your heart what is on His. Making disciples begins with evangelism. As one person put it, the objective of the Christian life is to populate heaven and depopulate hell." [15]

The important difference between a Christian and a disciple was pointed out at the 1983 Amsterdam International Conference for Itinerant Evangelists by Kalevi Lehtinen: "The word *Christian* emphasizes our *position* as members of God's family. The word *disciple* emphasizes the process: a disciple is a follower, a person who is in the process of learning . . . He is not only saved by Jesus Christ, but also controlled and used by Jesus Christ." [16]

Unfortunately, it is easier to measure a decision at a point in time than to measure the progress of discipleship, which occurs over a time period. It is more difficult to measure many small steps, which may be almost imperceptible, than one dramatic event which is clearly recognizable. Too often, however, the Adventist church has settled on outreach alone as the fulfillment of Christ's commission and measured its effectiveness by decisions gained. We have placed much more emphasis on the word "Go" than we have on the process of making disciples.

> We have placed much more emphasis on the word "Go" than we have on the process of making disciples.

Herein lies great danger. Evangelism that emphasizes decisions over disciples might actually destroy that which it has attempted to accomplish. Win Arn, for one, believes that this may have already occurred and that the very word "evangelism," appropriate in its correct understanding, may have become inappropriate in its application: "Today 'evangelism'—as widely practiced in American churches—is inhibiting the fulfillment of the Great Commission . . . I am finding that the very word evangelism is so closely associated with many ineffective and unproductive activities intended to Christianize the unconverted that even the use of the word creates obstacles in the minds of laity in most local churches. Perhaps a few generations from now the word can be reintroduced, when the inaccurate stigmas and stereotypes are gone. But for now, even the word is getting in the way of the process." [17]

Peter Wagner argues that in those churches where registering decisions alone is the end result of evangelism, "it is hard to justify continuing it. Why? Because only accomplishing the end—making disciples—can justify the means." [18] Oscar Thompson adds, "*Therefore, as you are going, disciple all nations, baptizing them* . . . We are good at teaching, and we are good at baptizing. But somehow we have lost our central theme. We are not very good at making disciples as we are going." [19]

Billy Graham's commentary on the fifteen affirmations, made at the 1983 Amsterdam conference on evangelism, states the problem in its proper perspective: "They [the evangelists] recognize their role as spiritual harvesters, but do little, if anything to preserve the results of their ministries.

They may accept that new Christians need to be nurtured, but are quite content to leave this to others. While it is true that other mature Christians will almost certainly have a part in this, the evangelist should not assume that it happens automatically. Converts (or "inquirers" as we call them) need encouragement and instruction from him. Evangelism is more than simply encouraging decisions for Christ. It is urging people to become disciples—followers—of Jesus Christ." [20]

Knowing the truth and being a disciple

A distinct, but subtle, difference must be maintained between justification (regeneration) and sanctification (conversion process), between baptism (the beginning) and discipling (the process and the goal). Failure to make this distinction lets the church assume erroneously that the two are identical or that discipleship occurs automatically or that it follows new birth naturally. Without such distinction, long-established members are often disappointed at the lack of maturity in the lives of new members. As a result, they mistakenly conclude that the spiritual struggles of the new members are due to insufficient instruction. [21]

Thus the "older" members feel that if appropriate instruction had been given, the new members would "fit" well into the church. This is a false assumption. Knowledge alone cannot ensure spiritual development, and spiritual struggle does not mean spiritual poverty. The experience of the church at Corinth shows that knowledge alone cannot guarantee spiritual maturity. While we must never abandon our love of truth, we must remember that knowledge alone is not the objective. Knowing the truth must produce a change in life, a transformation that comes from a love relationship with Jesus.

Now this concept stands squarely against the notion that those new believers who struggle were insufficiently prepared for baptism. The analysis of Engel and Norton on the role of "right teaching" in evangelical churches is applicable to Adventists as well: "Some would . . . assert that the amount of doctrinal knowledge one has is the best gauge of his spiritual maturity. On this assumption, the new believer thus would be cultivated primarily through straightforward doctrinal teaching and preaching. If doctrinal knowledge itself is the essence of spiritual maturity, however, then the evangelical church, especially in the United States, should be characterized by believers who are using their spiritual muscle to 'turn the world upside down.' " [22]

Actualizing God's will

The church has been called to evangelize! The great commission is the church's task and this task is not complete until new believers are actualizing the will of God in their choices and actions. Equipping newborn Christians for this task and guiding them in the process is follow-up. This is discipleship! "Evangelism involves taking people from the kingdom of Satan and placing them in the kingdom of Christ. Just as evangelism is analogous to putting plants out in a garden, so disciple building is analogous to tending a garden. An inexperienced gardener might feel a great sense of accomplishment in planting a tomato garden. But if he only planted new plants and neglected to care for the plants that already grew in his garden soon he would have problems. His tomato plants would either begin to die from lack of fertilizer or water, or they would be smothered by weeds or eaten by insects. On the other hand, if the gardener only tended his plants, not making any provision for planting more tomatoes the next season, he would also be without fruit. Evangelism and disciple building must work together. Each is essential to the other." [23]

Unless the process of integrating new members into the active life of the congregation is part of evangelistic planning, an unhealthy and potentially deadly dichotomy is set up, which differentiates between bringing new believers to Christ and establishing those new believers. The stabilization of new members must be as much an integral part of the process as is leading individuals to accept the Saviour. It is only when the new members themselves become active, reproducing disciples that the process has reached its completion—a completion, by the way, which begins the process all over again.

The product of an apple seed is ultimately another apple tree. The fruit of a disciple is another believer! Eddie Gibbs underscores this principle when he discusses regeneration and sanctification as part of the whole process. "The evidence of the presence of the Holy Spirit in a person's life is to be seen not primarily in sensational exploits but in Christlike character and conduct. His instantaneous work of regeneration is followed by His gradual, progressive work of sanctification." [24]

Gibbs points out that the fruit of a tree first identifies what type of tree it is and, then, states something about the health of the tree. Only when the maturing new believer produces fruit—and only when that fruit is observed as healthy—can we be certain that the process of new member assimilation is approaching its ideal. "The fruit is the evidence of the 'abundant life' which Jesus came to give (John 10:10). Such life cannot be contained by the tree, it must burst out in fruit." [25]

The church's ministry of discipling is not only the imperative of the great commission but also a factor in maintaining spirituality for those members who are already discipled. In other words, if believers are not involved in discipling others, their own discipleship is limited, lacking and losing ground rather than vital and growing. If those who walk in faith do not keep the mission of discipling clearly focused, they lose a vision for the very thing that will bring increased spirituality to their own lives.

Unreasonable expectations for new members lead some established members to forget their own process of sanctification and to conclude that all believers should arrive "prepackaged" mature. Insufficient developmental time is allowed for the newly born Christian to develop—for the fruits to grow. In our effort to make them "just like us," we even seem willing to have wax fruit glued onto the tree rather than wait for the genuine fruit to appear. Richard Neuhaus speaks of the church's role in the "process of being saved" and says, "The impulse to impose *the* Christian life-style or *the* model of ministry is wrongheaded. Unless it is restrained, it inevitably results in the 'unchurching' of Christians." [26]

Other established members, fearing that they will be perceived as attempting to impose too much on new members, tend to adopt an equally dangerous "hands-off" approach to new members. Benign neglect, they assume, will allow the new believer's spiritual life to develop naturally. Nothing could be farther from the truth. Notice George Peters' warning of this danger: "To hope that the convert will eventually grow out of his semi-paganism into a pure form of Christianity is not realistic. History gives little support to such hope. The opposite is far more likely. The New Testament clearly calls on the Christians to 'come out from among them and be separate' (2 Corinthians 6:17), and not to walk as the Gentiles do." [27]

> ~
> **You cannot teach an egg to fly before it is hatched.**
> ~

But some longer-established members ask, "Why can't this happen prior to baptism? Why can't we have maturity right from the moment the new members are added to the church books? Why can't the new members be sufficiently indoctrinated (instruction is equated with preparation in this didactical model) prior to their joining the church?" George E. Sweazey offers a helpful answer. "'As you have therefore received Christ Jesus the Lord, so walk ye in Him.' It must all start with receiving Christ Jesus as Lord. No amount of teaching or training can make a Christian out of someone who has not done that. You can't teach an egg to fly before it's hatched." [28]

We should not conclude that "flying" is unimportant. It is vital! It is urgent. It must be prioritized. But note its proper order. "*Evangelism* must not only bring people to look to Christ as Lord; it must also start them on their Christian walk." [29] Sweazey argues that the church's neglect of follow-up for discipleship is the great scandal of evangelism. When the church neglects its duty to nurture the new believer, it fails in its responsibility to Jesus who says, "Inasmuch as ye have done it to the least of these, my brethren, ye have done it unto me." He quotes Herschel Hobbs: "We have dipped them and dropped them. Evidence that other churches are doing the same is seen in the shocking figures on suspensions from membership. We abandon our new members to make their own way into the new life toward which they have turned, and as might be expected, an appalling proportion of them never make it. This does not have to happen. Most of those who join a church expect to remain as active members. Those who drop away have been disappointed. Things did not turn out as they had hoped. As a lapsed member said, 'I wish they had cared about me as much as they cared about my soul'. Part of our neglect comes from a mistaken theology. A person who has decided to take Christ as Lord is not by lightning from heaven suddenly given the knowledge and habits that a Christian needs. Only the Holy Spirit can make a person a Christian, but the Spirit works through the church, both in the calling and the establishing." [30]

The Christian walk within the church

Notice this development of the Christian walk as it occurs *within* the church in the New Testament. Making disciples and baptizing believers is followed by "teaching them to observe all that I have commanded" (Matt. 28:19-20). Those who turned to Christ on the day of Pentecost "devoted themselves to the apostles' teaching" (Acts 2:42). Although Apollos had ardently accepted Jesus, he urgently needed Priscilla and Aquila to take him aside and "expound to him the way" (Acts 18:26). This is the church's task! "The transformation of life into the image of Christ is personal, but not private. It is individual, but always in the context of a community of faith (1 John 1:3) . . . The individual requires the nurture of the church, and the church for its completeness requires the gifts of all the members. Transformation occurs in individuals, but in the context of community (1 Corinthians 12:12-26)." [31]

Developing disciples as a method of caring for new converts within the context of the congregation is a hallmark of growing churches. George Barna's study of what makes certain churches grow discovered that demonstrating a relevance of the church to the challenges of everyday life is essential and that this must occur within the church.

The church must consistently explore, describe, and demonstrate the relevance of the Christian faith for people. Unless adults understand in very real ways how and why Christianity is meaningful to life today, they will not make the kind of commitment that faith requires. [32]

Furthermore, notice where this demonstration and experience of relevance is to occur. "In all the growing churches studied, efforts were made to remind people that their responsibility was to *be* the church, not just to *attend* one." [33]

Adventist researchers Roger Dudley and Des Cummings, looking at the situation in the Adventist church, say: "Of what use is it to baptize new converts if we fail to incorporate them into responsible membership and they soon slip out 'the back door?' Is not a member preserved as valuable as a convert won? If we do not promote a strong spiritual internal growth within our congregations, we will soon find that we are working against ourselves. We may slip back faster than we progress forward. In the end we may find that we have not only not grown internally, but even the numerical growth that we so eagerly sought has eluded us. We have lost everything." [34]

> ⁓
> ## People must "be" the church, not just attend one.
> ⁓

William Martin's biography of Billy Graham, *A Prophet With Honor,* discusses this issue as the crux of evaluating crusade evangelism. He says: "As one who has long compared himself to the harvester who reaps what others have sown and cultivated, Billy Graham recognizes that the harvest, to be of significant use to any but scavengers, must be gathered into barns and protected against hostile elements. By his own criterion, then, it is disciple making rather than decision counting that must serve as the ultimate measure of an evangelist's accomplishment." [35]

According to Carl Wilson, Satan has tricked the church into divorcing evangelism from disciple building and into viewing the two as separate functions. "Where in the Scriptures do Jesus or the apostles separate the two ideas or debate one against the other? Evangelism is the process of winning men, enabling them to enter the kingdom of God. Disciple building is the process of teaching the new citizen how to obey the laws of the King and how to win and train others to do the same." [36]

The bottom line is this: The church is called to bring individuals to belief and to discipleship. The ultimate task of the church is "discipling."

Chapter 2

Nurturing Newborns

Jesus answered and said to him, Most assuredly, I say to you, unless one is born again, he cannot see the kingdom of God . . . Do not marvel that I said to you, "You must be born again" (John 3:3, 7, NKJV).

When Jesus described the conversion process to Nicodemus, it was not by accident that He selected the imagery of "born again" rather than words denoting human attainment or accomplishment. Furthermore, even among those words which He could have utilized to speak of a new start, Jesus selected "birth" for a specific reason. Jesus' conversation with Nicodemus "fits" other biblical passages that support a "family motif" in describing the process of becoming a disciple and a member of Christ's church.

Keeping this family motif in mind, note the following contemporary example that demonstrates the biblical imperative for assimilating new members as part of a whole process of conversion rather than viewing conversion as an event isolated from appropriate follow-up.

A number of years ago, my brother, John, met, fell in love with, and eventually married Pam. Their love relationship in marriage led them to desire children and, in fact, to conceive a child. The potential parents now entered into a time of development and waiting, known as gestation. Their own activities during these nine months expanded to involve classes about birth options, parenting skills, and the needs of newborns. Their joyful anticipation caused them to make a variety of careful and special preparations for the arrival of their child. Finally the day came when a daughter, Jana, was born. Their rejoicing was exceeded, if that were possible, by that of the whole family who welcomed the first grandchild on either side. This was a birth to be celebrated, and to this very day we still commemorate it!

Six weeks of eager waiting followed Jana's birth as we all anticipated the first holiday in which the entire family could be together with the new baby. When the holiday finally arrived, grandparents, aunts, and uncles were vying to be the first to hold the new baby and provide for her needs.

Although the infant was totally dependent upon adults for everything, and even though she chose generally annoying ways of expressing her needs (including crying, kicking and screaming, flailing about, and producing the most horribly smelly messes), someone was always there ready to meet her need. During this time of total dependency, however, Jana grew rapidly and experienced virtually everything that children normally encounter.

Now almost eighteen years have passed. Jana has grown into a lovely young woman. She is increasingly less dependent upon her parents to sustain her needs. She has learned to make basic choices which once were made for her. Her abilities continue to grow as she matures. No doubt she will eventually mature to the point that she will also establish her own love relationship within marriage and, most likely, bear children. This entire process might be diagramed as follows (although a circular model might be preferable to a linear model).

Husband and **Wife's**
Love Relationship
in **marriage**
Produces a **desire**
for Children
leading to conception
Gestation brings systematic
fetal **development** and
active parental **preparation**
Birth occurs at
appropriate time
as pain results in **joy**
The new **baby**
is **totally dependent**
even during **rapid growth**
Continued growth
leads to **maturity**
and eventual **marriage**

Family model

Although no analogy is perfect, if we choose this family model of love producing a desire for children, conception leading to a developmental gestation process which culminates in the birth of a totally dependent infant who rapidly grows and eventually matures into sharing a love relationship that bears offspring, we discover that the Bible not only allows for such an analogy but, in fact, these are the very images Jesus uses to teach this truth.

Therefore, even though we began with a parable from life today, this is not an "eisegetical" exercise of going to the Scriptures with a preconceived notion of hoping to read into the text some support. Rather, it is an exegetical realization of great truth that may have been largely ignored in previous attempts to justify our own preconceived notions of how conversion should take place and what should be expected of new believers.

For example, Scriptures clearly liken Jesus' personal love relationship with His church to that of a husband for his wife: "Husbands, love your wives, even as Christ also loved the church and gave Himself for it . . . that He might present it unto Himself a glorious church, not having spot, or wrinkle, or any such thing; but that it should be holy and without blemish. So ought men to love their wives as their own bodies . . . This is a great mystery; but I speak concerning Christ and the church" (Eph. 5:25, 27-28, 32).

> **The church must accept responsibility for newborn believers.**

Again and again the Bible pictures the role of the church toward the new believer as that of Christ's bride parenting those who have come to Him! Just as parents do not abandon a baby after birth but nourish and protect the child, so the church must assume responsibility for those who are born into God's family.

The apostle Paul spoke of his paternal relationship with the Corinthians. Paul had a fatherly concern for them that others could not possess (1 Cor. 4:14-15). He maintained an active communication with them, giving instructions about how they should live, serve, and teach in their church. As the human instrument who had led them into God's family, Paul looked beyond short-term results to growth, maturity, and true reproduction in their lives. He also described his ministry to new converts as that of a nurse who affectionately, gently, and faithfully cares for her children (1 Thess. 2:7).[37]

This is process. This takes time. This moves beyond event and concentrates on eventuality. Not only the decision, but what will come of that decision? What will the end result be? To an age that demands instantaneous results, Scripture describes a long-term process. Jesus compares the expansion of the kingdom through human conversions to the process by which a seed is planted, germinates, sprouts, matures, and bears fruit: "So is the kingdom of God, as if a man should cast seed into the ground; and should sleep, and rise night and day, and the seed should spring and grow up, he knoweth not how. For the earth bringeth forth fruit of herself; first the blade, then the ear, after that the full corn in the ear" (Mark 4:26-28).

Growth and fruit bearing

Birth and growth are well illustrated in Jesus' choice of words "born again" to describe the process of regeneration, which includes two specific steps–born of water and Spirit: "Verily, verily, I say unto thee, Except a man be born of water and of the Spirit, he cannot enter into the kingdom of God. That which is born of the flesh is flesh; and that which is born of the Spirit is spirit. Marvel not that I said unto thee, Ye must be born again" (John 3:5).

The apostle Paul expands this theme of "born of the water and of the Spirit" in Galatians, Colossians, and especially in Romans, chapters 6 through 8. The entrance into union with Christ envisioned by the Saviour's "born of the water" metaphor is picked up by Paul to describe baptism as a vital part of the process–but not the whole process! Note these passages: "For ye are all the children of God by faith in Christ Jesus. For as many of you as have been baptized into Christ have put on Christ" (Gal. 3:26-27). "Buried with Him in baptism, wherein also ye are risen with Him through the faith of the operation of God, who hath raised Him from the dead" (Col. 2:12). "Know ye not that so many of us as were baptized into Jesus Christ were baptized into His death. Therefore we are buried with Him by baptism into death; that like as Christ was raised up from the dead by the glory of the Father, even so we also should walk in newness of life" (Rom. 6:3-4).

Now, compare this with Paul's assertion as to how the newly baptized is to "walk in newness of life." Here is a key to understanding sanctification as "righteousness by faith." The walk of the Christian life after baptism must be empowered by the Holy Spirit just as surely as repentance and justification of the sinner must be by God's grace on our behalf before and at the point of baptism. It is our Saviour's work from start to finish!

"Likewise reckon ye also yourselves to be dead indeed unto sin, but alive unto God through Jesus Christ our Lord" (Rom. 6:11). "There is therefore now no condemnation to them which are in Christ Jesus, who walk not after the flesh, but after the Spirit" (Rom. 8:1).

Furthermore, the newborn believers cannot remain infants. It is necessary that they must grow. Their spiritual development must not be arrested. Note the following Scriptural passage and commentary provided by Keith Bailey: "'For though by this time you ought to be teachers, you have need again for someone to teach you the elementary principles of the oracles of God, and you have come to need milk and not solid food. For every one who partakes only of milk is not accustomed to the word of righteousness, for he is a babe. But solid food is for the mature, who because of practice have their senses trained to discern good and evil' (Heb. 5:12-14).

"The condition of prolonged spiritual infancy is, in most cases, the result of poor discipleship or of no discipleship at all. Converts are no more able to care for themselves than babies are able to care for themselves. Neglect of the new convert at this stage tends to make him a spiritual dropout or it locks him into permanent babyhood. The convert who was destined to be a stalwart servant of Christ and His church remains an infant in need of perpetual care." [38]

To conclude the biblical passages supporting this model, notice Jesus' own expectation for His followers to bear fruit: "Herein is my Father glorified, that ye bear much fruit; so shall ye be my disciples . . . Ye have not chosen me, but I have chosen you, and ordained you, that ye should go and bring forth fruit, and that your fruit should remain; that whatsoever ye shall ask of the Father in my name, He may give it unto you" (John 15:8, 16).

The goal, then, is fruit-bearing maturity. While it is one thing to have a baby born, it is quite another to see that baby grow, develop, and mature. The process is ongoing. Two-year-old children still need to have their diapers changed at times. They are not yet fully mature. They are still learning to walk and they still fall down and bruise their knees. At times they will need correction, loving and careful guidance, and discipline. So it is with new members. They need care, attention, love, correction, discipline. This is the church's responsibility. To do anything less would be child abuse!

Returning to our analogy, the biblical model becomes a clear teacher:

Husband and **Wife's Love Relationship** in **marriage**	**Christ** and **His church's Love Relationship** in **marriage** (His Bride)
Produces a **desire for Children**	Produces a **desire for fruit**
leading to conception	leading to evangelism
Gestation brings systematic fetal **development** and active parental **preparation**	**Gospel proclamation develops potential believers** and **prepares** the **church** to **nurture**
Birth occurs at appropriate time as pain results in **joy**	God's work of **Regeneration** evidences in **joy at New Birth** Born of Water = Baptism
The new **baby** is **totally dependent**	The **New Believer** is **totally dependent**

upon its parents	upon the church
even during **rapid growth**	even during **rapid spiritual growth**
Continued growth	**Continued spiritual growth**
leads to **maturity**	leads to **mature, fruit-bearing disciple**
and eventual **marriage**	**Born of Spirit = Sanctification process**

The process of discipleship

If this model demonstrates anything, it shows that the product of evangelism is the *process* of discipleship. A corporate executive once told his sales representatives that their time spent developing good relationships with established and potential customers was more important for the long-term success of their venture than making the sale at the moment. He concluded by saying, "The process is more important than the product." To paraphrase with regard to evangelism, *the process is the product!*

No wonder evangelism fails if it becomes separated from nurturing of the new believer. It would be more logical to assume that people come to Christ by chance than to assume that they are nurtured just because they are regenerated. Walter Henrichsen describes the nurturing, follow-up process: "Follow-up, then, is spiritual pediatrics. It has to do with the care and protection of the spiritual infant. It deals with the development of new babes in Christ from the time of their new birth until they grow and provide for themselves." [39]

John Stott offers three distinctions between regeneration and conversion, yet carefully maintains that they are inseparable. "Each belongs to the other as obverse and reverse of the same coin." [40] Note these three distinctions, particularly the third in which he quotes from John Owen's *Pneumatologia:*

"1. Regeneration is God's act, whereas conversion is man's. Regeneration is the peculiar work of the Holy Spirit who Himself infuses life into the dead. Conversion, on the other hand, is what we do when we repent and believe, albeit these two are also gifts from God.

"2. Regeneration is unconscious, whereas conversion is normally conscious. While the new birth itself is a mysterious work—'the wind blows where it wills, and you hear the sound of it, but you do not know whence it comes or whither it goes; so it is with everyone who is born of the Spirit'— nevertheless, its consequences are plain.

"3. 'The third difference between regeneration and conversion is that the former is an instantaneous and complete work of God, whereas the turn of repentance and faith which we call "conversion" is *more a process than an event'.* " [41]

Stott continues to expand this point, demonstrating the process by using this same motif of birth. Regeneration is instant, while conversion (or sanctification) continues forward from the point of regeneration. He says: "For though months of gestation precede it and years of growth follow it, birth itself is a crisis event. We are either born . . . [or] unborn, just as we are either alive or dead. Further, birth is a complete experience. Once born we can never be more born than at the first moment of emergence from the womb. So with the new birth. To quote John Owen . . . regeneration is 'not capable of degrees, so that one should be more regenerate than another. Every one that is born of God is equally so, though one may be more beautiful than another, as having the image of his Heavenly Father more evidently impressed on him, though not more truly. Men may be more or less holy; more or less sanctified; but they cannot be more or less regenerate.' "[42]

And where is the place for these newly regenerated believers, regardless of their level of sanctification, regardless of how "beautiful" they are, regardless of what they lack? The church! This may be a most difficult concept for Adventists. But this is New Testament ecclesiology that can transform our church. The reason many longtime members are disappointed when their expectations for spiritual development in new believers are not realized is based on equating the event of regeneration with the process of conversion and sanctification.

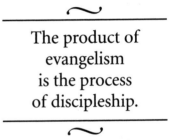

The product of
evangelism
is the process
of discipleship.

The difficulty in understanding this concept may be as much theological as practical. Unfortunately, however, theological confusion has devastating results when we apply it to the process of discipling new believers as the follow-up to evangelistic events. We try to teach eggs to fly before they are hatched.[43]

Our intent is to nurture newborn Christians, but we simply cannot see why they need so much care. We do not understand why they are so immature. We want evangelism to give birth to full-grown Christians. We wish new believers were sanctified at regeneration in order to excuse our lethargy or legitimize our reluctance to work at the hard task of discipling the newcomers.

The church must not view follow-up as an option that may be selected if there are those who feel called to minister to new believers. Follow-up to incorporate new believers is not an option; it is an imperative—an integral part of the whole process. Anything less than an all-out effort on behalf of the newborns is child abuse! It is criminal.

The church's task is not complete until new believers are actualizing the will of God in their choices and actions. Such an understanding of the theology of *assimilation as a process* will enable us to move toward practical applications based on valid expectations that "newborns" usually upset the status quo of the established family circle.

Rather than feeling great trauma when new believers struggle, the church should rejoice because these very struggles validate the new believers' experience as genuine. Engel and Norton say: "The key to growth and fruitfulness in the life of the Christian comes in the struggle to apply biblical teaching to the problems of everyday life. . . . Members, under their spiritual masks, are having some deep struggles in arriving at a lifestyle that conforms to the example Jesus gave. In reality, the existence of these problems and struggles is a positive sign that believers are taking their Christianity seriously. Their absence, on the other hand, implies an almost Pharisaical existence in which the believer has "arrived" at a comfortable, satisfying life that is outwardly Christian and orthodox but inwardly void of anything approaching Jesus' standards." [44]

Patterns in the life of the newborn

In fact, rather than being surprised or dismayed by these intrusions into the norm, we should learn to rejoice because it means things are normal and are progressing as they should. To return to our family analogy, several observable patterns will quickly emerge in the life of normal newborns that are applicable to new believers:

1. Arrival of the newborns completely upsets the status quo for the family. Established patterns of "how things ought to be" are quickly discarded.

2. Newborns utterly depend upon their parents for everything. Left alone, without their vital support, infants would quickly perish.

3. Newborns are totally self-centered, totally unaware of the fact that anyone else has needs, and totally expectant that their needs will be fully met by the family members.

4. Newborns usually express their demands in socially unacceptable methods—crying, kicking, screaming uncontrollably—because this is their only available communication option.

5. Newborns will regularly produce horribly smelly messes which are simultaneously offensive to the rest of the family (the bad news) as well as an indicator that life is progressing normally (the good news).

6. Newborns need consistent monitoring by the family to assure that gains in growth are occurring as they should and that harmful things are avoided.

7. Newborns are incapable of discernment and may readily ingest

something that could harm them as quickly as they would choose that which is beneficial.

8. Although newborns will quickly recognize their own caregivers, it is equally possible for them readily to accept nurture—or to receive abuse—from others.

9. When newborns arrive prematurely, efforts are redoubled and heroic measures are taken to save their lives. Failure to do less or to properly nurture any infant is criminal.

10. Newborns will experience rapid but sporadic growth. Responsibility for providing appropriate nourishment and consistent nurture belongs to parents, not to the infant.

11. Maturity is a process of time, but does not automatically occur with the passing of time. Parents must teach even simple tasks repeatedly as they work toward teaching the children eventually to make their own decisions.

The parenting task begins in earnest once the child is born. If the infant is neglected or abused, the fault is not the child's. After birth, come years of careful nurture and training to ensure that children grow and develop to mature adults when they can marry and assume responsibility for their own families.[45]

Parents are not surprised at anything babies do because "anything can be expected!" The responsible parent does not despair when a child makes an unwise choice or acts imprudently. The responsible parent does not shun the disobedient child whose maturity fails to equal an adult's. Instead, responsible parents train, coach, empathize, reason, model, teach, and supervise their children to the point of maturity. Note Carl M. Sweazy's analysis: "It is a mistake to imagine that conversion, though unquestionably genuine, is the finished work and accomplishes everything to be desired. Suppose a baby is born in the delivery room at the hospital, and as soon as the birth is a certainty, both doctors and nurses walk out of the delivery room leaving the mother and her new born baby as though there was no more to be done? . . . We might properly ask the question, What man is there who will lead a soul to Christ and not go on to guide that soul into a fruitful life that honors Christ?"[46]

Too often the church wishes to give birth to full-grown adults rather than deal with the challenges of newborns. Producing such newborn adults is a spiritually impossible task. But that does not slow the search for that "new and improved" technique that guarantees problem-free converts. Consequently, when the new believers fail to measure up, they are often excluded or made to feel like second-class citizens either because of their newness or because of their insufficient spiritual maturity, or both! Furthermore, if these new believers experience such isolation, they often become discouraged by the intolerance of the church at the very moment they most need encouragement and nurture. These new believers are not bad, they are babies!

Notice how this concept stands squarely against the notion that new members who struggle are lacking genuine regeneration. In fact, rather than being dismayed when new members struggle, the church should expect that Satan will especially attack newborns immediately after their baptism and thus it can anticipate how to meet their needs in this time of spiritual warfare.

It is far more instructive than coincidental that Jesus experienced His most severe temptations and engaged in protracted spiritual battle immediately following His own baptism. Walter Henrichsen says: "It is one thing to engage the enemy in combat and set the captives free, but it is altogether another thing to spend the necessary time with a new convert to see that he grows and matures into the likeness of Jesus Christ." [47]

Ben Campbell Johnson points out that in the process of trans-formation a person experiences moments of awareness, redecision, and response followed by periods of growth and development. These are times of spiritual struggle: "The experience of regeneration creates a new relationship with God which manifests itself as joy, peace, and the unity of one's being. But this new life does not develop without distraction and struggle. The old life of alienation immediately challenges this new creation (Romans 7:21-25; Galatians 3:1-5). For some persons, the new life of the Spirit breaks into consciousness with such dramatic force that they feel separated completely from the old life of estrangement. But in the course of time, old habits return with their perverse imaginations and evil lusts. Caught in this contradiction, they realize that the new center has not created experientially a whole new person. This inner struggle between the old and the new forms the matrix within which the work of sanctification takes place." [48]

When the long-established members express disappointment at the lack of maturity in the lives of new members, they essentially say that they do not wish to parent. Unreasonable expectations lead established members to seek that which cannot occur—instantaneous sanctification. Engel and Norton say, "The decision process does not cease when the believer has become spiritually alive. Rather the Holy Spirit now undertakes sanctification, which results in a growing conformity over a lifetime to the image of Christ." [49]

The apostle Peter says, "As newborn babes, desire the sincere milk of the word, that ye may grow thereby" (1 Pet. 2:2). This growth takes place within the family structure of Christ's bride—the church. It is the church's work of "familying."

Chapter 3

Conserving the Catch

Again, the kingdom of heaven is like a dragnet that was cast into the sea and gathered some of every kind, which, when it was full, they drew to shore; and they sat down and gathered the good into vessels, but threw the bad away. So it will be at the end of the age. The angels will come forth (and) separate the wicked from among the just (Matt. 13:47-49, NKJV).

Adventists doing the work of angels! Many times that is expressed in charitable, self-denying, and benevolent actions. But with regard to new believers, too often we do what Jesus says must be reserved for the day of judgment and for angels who will serve as God's agents. We want to judge. We want to sort the catch. We want to discard the bad. We want to stop fishing and start evaluating the catch.

Jesus took the illustration of the dragnet from everyday life—a large net, pulled by boats, gathering all in its path. If it were possible for the dragnet to select only that which is edible, clean, and palatable, then the eventual process of sorting, preserving, and discarding would be unnecessary. But such is not the function of the dragnet. It gathers all that it sweeps across and all remain together until the time of evaluation (judgment).

This parable is not a depiction of one-to-one, personal evangelism; it is far more inclusive. Chaney and Lewis say: "Most modern evangelicals who, if they fish at all, fish for sport, have misunderstood the figure Jesus used. They think of a fisherman as a man who uses a rod, line, and lure. Fishing is a one-on-one proposition. In this way, this text has been used to encourage modern Christians to become personal evangelists. The early disciples fished with nets. Fish were in schools, hopefully, certainly not caught one at a time. Growing churches have captured that vision. They have learned how to fish with nets." [50]

Two lessons are clear from this parable. First, God expects great numbers to be gathered in. Second, He expects the church to cope with the reality that both good and bad will be caught. We will first discuss the issue of good and bad remaining together and then deal with potential conflicts over the issue of numbers.

The good and the bad

Like the parable of the wheat and tares (Matt. 13:24-30), Jesus' parable of the dragnet demonstrates that both good and bad will remain together until the end of the world. These two parables also avoid a separatism that prevents the people of God from associating with the people of the world. We are to be in the world, but not of the world.

Unlike our theological models of developing disciples and nurturing newborns, this parable does not deal with any transition from bad to good or from good to bad, but simply asserts that both exist together in the same environment. That environment is the church. In fact, Jesus clearly teaches that it is the role of the church to nurture new believers more than to evaluate them. Peter Wagner says, "In the early stages of growth it is sometimes difficult to tell true disciples from counterfeits. But that judgment is not usually the responsibility of the evangelist who is concerned more with discipling than perfecting." [51] The church's role is to take that new believer on to full discipleship and perfection of character.

Jesus does not vision the church as a "holier than thou" club that stands over against the rest of the world. Just as He ate with publicans and sinners, so His disciples will move and live among people who believe as well as those who disbelieve and behave badly.

The dragnet allows the understanding of variety among sinners. "Men are all alike sinners, but not sinners alike." [52] Some of those sinners, and a good deal of their misbehavior, will be exhibited within the milieu of the congregation. Of course, much of this misbehavior will occur in the lives of new believers (those who have recently been dragged in by the dragnet). If we understand the implications of nurturing newborns, we would expect this energetic misbehavior. And if we understand the concept of discipling, we would approach this misbehavior so as to turn the individual toward appropriate behavior and fruitful discipleship.

However, if the intolerance of older members rushes the church to the task of judgment, the all-too-frequent result is apostasy. Dudley and Cummings call it *the ogre of apostasy.* "Of all the ugly words in the Adventist vocabulary, the most horrible is surely 'apostasy.' It brings a cold chill and connotes a hopeless dread." [53]

Apostasy is such an operative dread that Adventists from the local congregation to the widest reaches of church organization measure evangelistic success or failure by apostasy. For example, a typical reaction of church members to an evangelistic event will not be so much rejoicing in the new members who have joined the church as it will be a subtle (and sometimes not so subtle) probing to determine "how many actually stuck!"

This preoccupation with "who stuck" is evident at every level of our denomination. For example, although statisticians in the Department of

Archives at the Adventist world headquarters have not developed adequate methods for determining and reporting those converts who have been developed to full discipleship, we have an accurate and well-developed methodology for reckoning those who have apostatized. Furthermore, our reporting mechanism compounds the problem by reporting annual apostasies as a percentage of that year's accessions rather than as a percentage of the total membership. Note the negative perception this produces: If a church of 100 members adds 24 new believers and loses six by apostasy, the statistics will report an apostasy rate of 25 percent (dropouts as a percentage of new accessions) rather than reporting an apostasy rate of just less than 5 percent (dropouts as a percentage of all members—the base group from which they "dropped out").

Is it any wonder that the perception of Adventist members in general toward evangelism has soured to the point that many congregations have concluded—and their boards voted— that "evangelism just isn't worth the effort when you 'lose' so many any-way!" Fear of failure becomes so pervasive that inertia is the response. Following this line of reasoning, congregations become more intent on avoiding any loss than they do on gaining new believers. One small conference presented a triennial report in which no accessions had

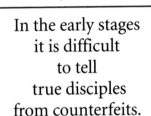

In the early stages it is difficult to tell true disciples from counterfeits.

occurred—absolutely zero new members. Rather than expressing remorse, they expressed their great joy that not one had been lost by apostasy! They rejoiced that they had not been "forced to remove anyone from the books." Now the fact that we "shoot ourselves in the foot" (some have suggested that we are shooting ourselves in the head) with this mechanism for reporting statistics does not mean that if we chose the alternative method of reporting apostasy as a percentage of membership, we would resolve our problem. The challenge is not statistical reporting, the challenge is people—thousands of individuals who have become alienated from the church. Dudley and Cummings state: "Scattered throughout North America are scores of thousands—perhaps hundreds of thousands—of ex-Seventh-day Adventists. In some communities their numbers may approach that of the active membership. They appear in all walks of life, including government, show business, and prison. Their presence is the plague spot on the Adventist mission." [54]

The trauma of statistics

Statistics document the extent of this trauma. In the twenty years between 1969 and 1989, over a quarter million members (253,938) were officially removed (and not because of death) from the membership of Adventist churches just in North America. That is more than one third of total North American membership. To put it another way, an equivalent of 253 one-thousand-member churches have disappeared. Myron Widmer, a former associate editor of the *Adventist Review,* says: "Backsliders, church dropouts, inactive members, whatever we call them, cause us pain. It's the side of our church that we whisper about but find difficult to talk about publicly, for by admitting that backsliders exist, we speak of failure. Whether it's ours or theirs, it's still failure. And failure is hard to swallow in any line, particularly by a church that senses a last-day prophetic calling and wants to be seen as successful, as growing, as friendly, as sharing the true gospel of Christ." [55]

> Attendance at spiritual functions builds spirituality and absence destroys spirituality.

Widmer points out that while some have chosen to leave because of doctrinal differences, disagreements over standards, or other issues, many have left because of lack of friends, boredom, loneliness, alienation, inadequate spiritual food, or conflict with fellow believers. Obviously these figures and the reasons why people leave should drive those strategies which will be developed in later chapters.

However, these statistics, appalling as they are, reveal only part of the challenge. Attendance figures suggest that only about 50 percent of our North American members attend worship services. Even considering that many are sick, too old to attend, or may be out of town for the weekend, the "active" membership still may be only 65 percent of those whose names are on the membership. This is an important issue, however, because attendance at spiritual functions builds spirituality and absence destroys spirituality. It was a great asset to the embryonic church to have her converts continue steadfastly in the apostles' doctrine and in attendance at the daily meetings in the temple. [56]

In response to Widmer's editorial and accompanying articles on former and inactive members, about 40 such individuals who had left the church shared their stories with the *Adventist Review*. Editor William Johnsson shared some of those responses in a subsequent issue: "I think these letters are important, but they are painful. They arise from a variety of backgrounds and feelings, and could be misused—I certainly do not want to nudge any reader to join the 'missing.' After considerable thought and prayer I have decided to share a selection of these letters with the church because I think they can serve a redemptive purpose. As you read them, ask yourself: Are the writers' observations true? If so, what changes should my church make? What might I do to help? These letters might be used as the basis for discussion . . . They can help us see ourselves as others see us, and thereby move the church closer to God's ideal. A second reason leads me to share these letters: The path of healing and reclamation first requires that we listen to those who hurt. That holds even when we do not agree with everything they say." [57]

Can you imagine the pain such letters cause, especially in view of the Adventist claim to being the remnant people with "the truth"? It is painful even to ask, "Why would someone choose to leave?" much less to be confronted with answers that identify the remaining members as contributors to the exit. Widmer comments: "But whatever the causes, two things are certain. The back door still swings, and the solutions lie more in our laps than we might dare to think, or practice." [58]

While apostasy is not unique to Seventh-day Adventists, it is particularly acute for a church whose members too often hold an emotional view of salvation by association (membership on the church books). This view is not rooted in our theology but in the historically isolationist sub-culture of Adventism that nurtures such a position. In fact, feelings in this regard are so strong that wise pastors have abandoned attempts to remove from the church books those children or relatives of longtime members, despite the reality that these children or relatives may make no profession of belief in any regard or, in some cases, even have chosen to affiliate with other denominations.

On the other hand, without the emotional attachment of family, heritage, parents, or other relatives, there is often a rush to "clean up the books" by removing those who have become discouraged or distant from a congregation they once willingly and joyfully embraced. Dudley and Cummings point out that such variables in attitudes on the part of the church itself present inadequate understandings of the issue: "Apostasy as a variable is difficult to interpret. The steps a person takes that lead him to reject his relationship with Christ and the church are usually gradual and occur over an extended period of time. A gap exists between the time that a member turns away from the church in heart and the point where the congregation actually drops his/her name. Therefore, we must observe caution in relating apostasy to other attitudes and behaviors, since the real variable may be *dealing* with apostasy, rather than the actual disaffiliating process." [59]

Therefore, any attempt to provide appropriate care for new converts must deal seriously with how we treat those who do not measure up to our expectations. A great deal of the problem is theological. We have tended to emphasize the role of Christ's bride, the church, as being spotless and without wrinkle to the exclusion of other biblical models that describe the church as a caring, sharing, and mutually growing atmosphere where new believers associate with those who have progressed farther in sanctification and with others who have barely made it off the beginner's mark.

It's important, therefore, that new believers should be encouraged to focus their lives on Jesus. If they look elsewhere, they will be sorely disappointed. If they look to those members who, over the process of years of spiritual growth (sanctification), have grown so Christlike, they might be tempted to conclude that they could never arrive at such a lofty level of holiness and thus give up before even beginning the Christian walk. On the other hand, if the new members look to those who have been in the church for long years but have experienced little transformation, then the new members might conclude that there is nothing to spiritual growth and thus abandon the faith without allowing the Holy Spirit to impact their lives.

Part of the challenge is how to view the church. Far too often Adventists have viewed the church as a museum where those specimens who have "arrived" are carefully displayed. This might well correlate to the "fortress" mentality which is described so well by Jerry Cook.[60] This view stands in sharp contrast to an alternative—the church as a force—which emphasizes the church's ministry and impact on the world around it as being more important than maintaining institutions which have been established. A vastly preferable alternative to the "fortress" or "museum" model is to view the church as a medical center where hurt and ailing individuals are first rescued from the immediacy of their trauma, rehabilitated to health, and then trained (i.e. a school of nursing) to care for others.

So what does the parable of the net tell us? Whatever the net drags in will be sorted; but this sorting is reserved for the day of judgment. The sorting cannot and must not become the function of the church. Jesus called His followers to become "fishers of men." The purpose of the fishermen, boats, and net is to catch the catch and to hold the catch. These activities cannot be halted mid-process in order to evaluate the catch or to discard the unsuitable for fear that the bad fish will contaminate the boat or the fishers.

The probability that some new believers will choose to leave the fellowship of the church is sad enough without the added potential that others will feel driven away by coldness, indifference, exclusiveness, and a judgmental attitude of superiority by those who have been longer "in the way."

Adventists too often have an unhealthy fear of those who would choose to leave our fellowship (which too often becomes a self-fulfilling prophecy) coupled with the potential of a superiority complex that encourages a pernicious spiritual haughtiness based on a gnostic-like attitude which equates "knowledge of the truth" with spiritual maturity and thus relegates those with inferior knowledge (i.e. new believers) to a second-class status.

Of course, there will always be those who choose to walk away from a church family in which they have been welcomed and affirmed. It is healthy regularly to remind ourselves that coming to Christ does not negate the new believers' free choice or eliminate individual preference. They may choose to abandon the church or even faith in Christ. At the same time, it is unfortunate if we allow this reality to predispose us to assume that all converts will quickly exit.

Why members leave

Adventist administrator Bruce Johnston edited a series of articles on "myths" regarding the church and addressed this issue specifically in his article, "All New Converts Soon Leave." Challenging this "myth," Johnston says, "The criticism of public evangelism can be devastating in two ways: First it can turn a church against evangelism and, secondly, it is most disheartening to pastors and evangelists who are bringing people to the Lord and into the church." [61]

> New members with friends stay; those without friends do not stay.

Johnston points out that research demonstrates that the methodology of recruiting new members or the length of the process that leads to a spiritual decision has much less to do with their retention rate than the atmosphere into which the new believer is introduced and the determination of the congregation to conserve the converts. He reviews a study of 204 individuals who joined an Adventist church over a four-year period in which 75.9 percent remained within the church and became active members. The study showed that there are factors in retention which have little or nothing to do with the preparation process and, instead, were most impacted by what happened to the new believer within the first half-year of fellowship. "The real factor was whether they knew six or eight people in the church within the first six months of membership. Those who knew people stayed; those who do not, did not stay." [62]

In 1989, Charles E. Bradford, then president of the North American Division of Seventh-day Adventists, researched and wrote on the issue of inactive and former members. Bradford points out that "one of the most widely held myths about dropouts is that they are the result of quick, high pressure public evangelism." The facts are just the opposite. "In fact, half of them grew up in Adventist homes and only one in seven came into the church through public evangelism. Four out of five spent more than two months in preparation for baptism, and the majority have attended church regularly for six years or longer. The method of evangelism or conversion has little to do with whether the person will or will not drop out of the church." [63]

However, Bradford's study reveals a significant constant with regard to dropouts. One's age is a powerful predictor. Nearly half the dropouts are in the 20-35 year age group, and another quarter are in the 36-50 year age bracket. Bradford quotes Jerry W. Lee, a researcher at Loma Linda University: "The church is losing its younger members." [64]

In another study, Dudley and Cummings cite interview surveys of 120 former or inactive members. This study gives excellent insight into their assimilation (or lack of assimilation) process and demonstrate that their experiences within the church exhibit certain traits:

"*Pre-baptismal Instruction:* 67 percent felt their pre-baptismal instruction to have been thorough or very thorough. Another 18 percent regarded their instruction as adequate. This is a total of 85 percent who believe they received adequate to thorough instruction.

"*Length of Pre-baptismal Process:* 31 percent studied the church's teachings from three to eleven months. Sixteen percent spent less than two months examining Adventist beliefs. Virtually all generally considered their baptismal instruction good in terms of depth and length of time of study.

"*Church Involvement:* 63 percent became only nominally involved once they were in the church. They participated in the church only through either regular or irregular worship attendance. Forty-eight percent reported a warm fellowship in the congregation, but another 48 percent felt different degrees of discomfort with other members. Generally speaking, former members did not become fully involved in the church's programs and ministries and were about equally divided in their recollections of the church's fellowship atmosphere.

"*Determining Factors in Leaving:* A lack of fellowship was the strongest factor influencing personal decisions to leave the church. Dissatisfaction with the worship and programming or the influence of non-member friends or relatives also had significant impact. Former members reported feelings of frustration, relief, and bitterness during the process of leaving. Other factors included personal failure to keep church standards or teachings, marital or family problems, the influence of other individuals, or conflict with pastors or other members.

"*Efforts to Reclaim Former Members:* Congregations did little to reclaim former members. Only 50 percent said that the pastor visited them and even fewer (34 percent) mentioned that a church member had come to see them. The general perception was that few church members or leaders cared enough to try to prevent them from leaving.

"*Post-Membership Attitudes:* Very few had joined other denominations after leaving the Adventist church. Of those who responded to the question about what could have been different in their experience with the church, nearly all gave answers suggesting more loving, consistent supportive relationships with other members.

~

Lack of fellowship
is the
strongest factor
influencing decisions
to leave
the church.

~

"*Reclamation Potential:* Former members appeared mainly undecided or pessimistic about their chances of becoming members again. Only 10 percent expressed any hope of joining the Adventist church once again although 43 percent indicated that no real obstructions existed except, possibly, their having no desire to return. Some former members also counted their current lifestyle as incompatible with church teachings. About 47 percent indicated their spiritual experience as either very good or, at least growing, while 37 percent said their relationship with Christ was either very weak or nonexistent." [65]

To summarize: while there are a variety of reasons why people exit the Adventist church, generally these reasons stem more from interpersonal relationships, or the lack thereof, than from doctrinal or lifestyle differences. While we would prefer to believe that the reasons people leave are more complex than they are, the essential conclusion must be that somehow we are failing to incorporate new believers into the fellowship of the congregation.

Ellen White counsels: "Those who have newly come to the faith should be patiently and tenderly dealt with, and it is the duty of the older members of the church to devise ways and means to provide help and sympathy and instruction for those who have conscientiously withdrawn from other churches.[66] The church has a special responsibility laid upon her to attend to these souls who have followed the first rays of light they have received; and if the members of the church neglect this duty, they will be unfaithful to the trust that God has given them." [67]

The challenge of apostasy

In discussing the challenge of apostasy among new converts, John W. Fowler quotes Roland Leavell, for years president and professor of evangelism at New Orleans Baptist Theological Seminary, who writes somewhat satirically about those who join churches: "Five percent do not exist, 10 percent cannot be found, 20 percent never pray, 25 percent never read the Bible, 30 percent never attend church services, 40 percent never give to any cause, 50 percent never go to Sunday school, 60 percent never go to church Sunday night, 70 percent never give to missions, 80 percent never go to prayer meetings, 90 percent never have family worship, 95 percent never win a soul to Christ." [68]

Fowler then adds, "Blame for the problem of apostasy is aimed in a number of different directions, with very little being done within the Seventh-day Adventist church to come to grips with a situation that should demand the attention of the entire church." [69]

In the early 90s, the North American Division of the Adventist church established a "think tank" whose responsibilities included looking at every phase of evangelistic endeavor. The first major recommendation of the committee was to launch an all-out effort to reclaim our inactive and former members. Our Marietta church was designated as the "pilot project" congregation in North America to test the proposals this committee has developed for reclaiming former and inactive members. Our church board, in voting its participation in this pilot project, viewed it as an integral part of our effort to appropriately assimilate members and saw this as a potential learning experience to help us avoid losing others. We were determined to express God's love, acceptance, and forgiveness in such a way that we became intentional in our expressions of concern rather than accidental or incidental. We intentionally chose to include former members as well as new believers rather than to exclude them. We built them up rather than tearing them down. We actively encouraged and nurtured them rather than discouraging them by inattention. We talked to them rather than about them. In Jesus' name, we chose to love them for who they are rather than despising them for what they lack.

> We talked to them rather than about them. We chose to love them for who they are.

Another helpful suggestion for our entire denomination was to give recognition and statistical acknowledgment to those who were actively attempting to prevent loss of new members and to reclaim those who have become inactive. If stemming the flow of discouraged and disgruntled members from the church is such a vital ministry, then we need creative methods to recognize those pastors and congregations who are attempting to deal with the issue.

Dudley and Cummings suggest a broadened approach to statistical reporting which includes the prevention of apostasy. They give an example from the sports world which, with the development of the relief pitcher as a specialist, necessitated a new baseball statistic—the save. If the relief pitcher can prevent the game from being lost, he is credited with a "save." Church statisticians keep careful records of accessions and typically recognize pastors successful in this area through statistical reports. But if pastors reclaim or disciple those who are inactive but have not been dropped from membership, they have no way to report this ministry. Thus, human nature dictates that pastors with a multiplicity of duties will direct their energies toward that which is "counted" and may find it easy to neglect that which is "ignored." [70]

Therefore, even though the primary focus of this chapter, and for that matter this entire book, is avoiding the loss of new members because of inadequate assimilation processes, it is important to remember that we can make a difference in the lives of our former and inactive members if we allow the Spirit to work in our lives. The same principles which will keep someone within the fellowship of the church will reclaim others. Widmer says, "When someone is getting divorced, or gives birth to an illegitimate child, or loses his job, or struggles with drinking, we should uncondemningly welcome that person. Too often we make him feel unwelcome, condemned, and rebuffed by silence or nonverbal avoidance. We can prevent the departure of many and we must. And we can and must actively search for the 'lost,' listen to them, and possibly reclaim them, both within and without our church walls. Not with a sense of superiority, for we are sinners too, but with the humbleness wrought by the sense that we are nothing but for the forgiving grace of God . . . The backslidden, church dropouts, missing or inactive members certainly aren't faceless creatures to most of us. They're our family, our friends, our fellow members. They deserve our best efforts today." [71]

To do less than we can to preserve those whom the Lord has given us would be worse than a tragedy for the church. It would be disobedience to Christ's command to fish for humanity. This preservation process is the church's work of conservation!

~ Part II ~

Strategies for Keeping New Members

Applying theology in the real world is simultaneously the great need and the great challenge for the church. When Jesus called for the church to be "in the world, but not of the world," He envisioned that what the church believed would be lived out in how its members acted.

Thus, Jesus' measurement for discipleship is based more on the attitudes that exist between church members than on theological orthodoxy—"By this shall all men know that you are my disciples, if you love one another" (John 13:35). This is not a call, however, for poor theology. Rather it is an invitation—a command if you will—to demonstrate theological orthodoxy in the crucible of the real world and in daily living.

We must also understand that living in today's "real" world calls for strategies that meet today's real needs. George Barna says: "Clearly, the Christian Body cannot hope to have much of an impact if we respond in the same ways we have in the past. These are new challenges, demanding creative, unique responses. The solutions that worked ten or even five years ago will fail in the coming decade. We are being confronted with a new wave of obstacles and opportunities. After careful study of our options, and discerning the mind of God, we must tailor new strategies to address this new environment." [72]

Demographic changes demand strategy changes. The great demographic phenomena today is the baby boomer generation's passing mid-life and the essential changes in society this has brought. For example, only 15 percent of today's families fit the traditional model of the nuclear family; 70 percent of mothers with young children now work outside the home; 45 percent of all households are headed by a single adult; 25 percent of parents have only one child; and another 25 percent of couples will have no children at all. "Church ministries designed for the needs of the sixties will not work in the eighties and nineties. While the church's message should never change, her methods must do so frequently. We must deal with society as it is, not as we hoped it might be." [73] Especially as we move into the new century, we must learn to meet the real-life challenges of today's society with new and invigorating strategies, rather than relying on assumptions and methods of the past.

> While the church's message should never change, her methods must do so frequently.

One of the greatest challenges facing the church in dealing with reality is our own self-image. Frank Tillapaugh says, "We are heir to a mentality that is basically defensive. In fact, it's not too strong to say that we have retreated to our fortresses with a disabling, deep-seated inferiority complex. Subtly the message has come through that the world out there is modern while we are old-fashioned. The world is seen as moving too quickly; it's too affluent, too educated, too sophisticated to be interested in biblical Christianity. In effect, we are ashamed of the gospel of Jesus Christ. We do not believe that the world could possibly want or need what we have . . . (The) average local church with its modest facilities needs to get the message loud and clear. 'Believe it or not, they really do need us out there.' " [74]

In Part II, we shall view three long-understood essentials that new members need from the church as they begin the Christian life and see how these essentials are interdependent and build upon each other. These principles may be timeless, but their implementation demands appropriate applications for today's "real world." Thus, a correct understanding of these essentials should drive strategies which will impact what the church does to, for, and with new members.

The ultimate benefit for the new believers would be for a congregation to utilize these strategies to develop a wide smorgasbord of options which they would then apply and offer as needed in the individual situation. To paraphrase the apostle Paul, the church would then "become all things to all people that by all means some might be preserved." This means appropriate approaches to today's predominant group—both baby boomers plus generation X. We must find ways to attract the newest generations without alienating the graying ones. "If we want to minister to today's society, we must speak to baby boomers in ways and words they can both accept and understand. We must be willing to 'become all things to all men'—in this case, all 76 million of them." [75]

Sharon Cress underlines three essential ingredients that are necessary for new members both to remain and to thrive within the church family:

"1. He/she must be able to articulate the doctrines of his/her faith.

"2. He/she must have friends (church growth studies are showing the necessary number to be six to eight) within the congregation.

"3. He/she must become involved in meaningful group activities."[76]

While theoretically it is possible to have a modicum of adherence with only two of these three ingredients functioning in the life of new members, reducing the experience of the new believers to only one of these three essential factors almost guarantees that they will depart.

> ∼
> ─────────────────
> We must find ways
> to attract the
> newest generations
> without alienating
> the graying ones.
> ─────────────────
> ∼

In the next three chapters, we will expand these three essentials of articulating beliefs, having friends, and being involved in meaningful activities as the basis for developing strategies aimed at more effectively keeping new members.

Although the primary emphasis will be on keeping new believers, another benefit will be in developing strategies that integrate new transfer members into the life of their newly chosen congregation as well. After all, even though the new transferees may be well able to articulate their beliefs, initially they most surely will be without friends and may never become involved in meaningful group activities unless the church has developed intentional strategies toward this accomplishment.

Chapter 4. The Opening of a Closed Community. An application of the theological imperatives discussed in Part I. The emphasis is for new members not only to be fully instructed in doctrine, but also to become fully discipled into a denominational subculture that has too often closed and isolated itself from society.

Chapter 5. Meaningful Relationships for Body Life. An application of the theological imperatives discussed in Part I . The emphasis is on the need for new members not only to be thoroughly instructed in the faith, but also to be seriously bonded to other believers in both spiritual discovery and accountability.

Chapter 6. New Jobs for New Members. An application of the theological imperatives discussed in Part I. The emphasis is on the need for new members not only to be fully integrated in true fellowship, but also to be fully employed as useful servants of the King.

Chapter 4

The Opening of a Closed Community

If the dissemination of information alone were sufficient to accomplish conversion, then Seventh-day Adventists, of all people, ought to be spiritual giants. With our numerous publishing ventures and worldwide network of literature evangelists, the Adventist church is the best thing that has happened to paper since the government talked people into taking it for money.

The ability to articulate personal beliefs—to have a theological basis for a belief system and to understand its biblical focus—is essential, of course. But it would be inappropriate to conclude that knowledge alone is sufficient. Perhaps this has been the great lack in Adventist evangelism—over-reliance on correct theology as the essential ingredient for attracting and incorporating individuals into the church without appropriate regard for the sociological factors of friendship and involvement that must also accompany doctrinal understanding.

Adventists prize the truth. In fact, love of theological correctness has been historically expressed with this very phrase—"the truth"—to describe the entire subcultural phenomena of the Seventh-day Adventist church. Our pride in theological accuracy and orthodoxy combined with a distinctively conservative lifestyle (scrupulous observance of Sabbath; no alcohol, tobacco, or "unclean" foods, if not outright vegetarianism; no theater, movies, novels, dancing; limited jewelry or makeup; limited extravagance possible when a distinctly high percentage of income is given to the church or utilized in educating children in parochial schools from preschool through university, etc.) has often produced a closed society into which we ostensibly welcome new believers but, practically, make it difficult for them to join.

Dangers of communalism

Adventists have often fostered what John R. W. Stott describes as a "disastrous development" called *communalism,* which is "the rise of a

Christian community which, instead of being scattered throughout the non-Christian community as salt and light, becomes isolated from it as a distinct cultural entity on its own." [77] This is evidenced by Adventist communities that have sprung up around educational institutions, publishing houses, medical facilities, organizational headquarters, or other types of Adventist entities. Now all is not bad in these communities. There is much to recommend the pleasant atmosphere, the safe, secure environment, and the separation from "worldly influences" that is available in such communities. However, to the extent that such communities (Angwin, Berrien Springs, Collegedale, College Place, College View, Cooranbong, Loma Linda, La Sierra, Salisbury Park, Stanborough Park, etc., are the present-day offspring of Battle Creek or Takoma Park) fail to integrate Adventist believers into the life and world view of those to whom we minister, we have added to an isolationist "communalism" more than we have preserved piety. Or worse, we have actually come to equate piety with isolationism. As one wag said it, "Adventists are like manure. Spread 'em around, they do a lot of good. Pile 'em together, they stink!"

Impious humor aside, however, the very survival of Adventist growth among Anglo North Americans may depend upon our ability to break out of this "communalism." Donald McGavran and Win Arn discuss the history of the Swedish Baptists in North America, who grew chiefly among Swedes until the late 1930s when they saw a new vision of what Christ wanted for them. Then they realized they were living in the midst of multitudes of unreached people who were not Swedish Americans, and they resolved to cease concentrating on just those of Swedish background and to win individuals from all backgrounds. They grew from forty thousand in 1940 to more than one hundred thousand in 1976 and projected that they would double again within the next ten years. [78]

Adventist church growth is changing rapidly. The movement was founded in the United States among an Anglo constituency and has historically been largely Anglo and, for the most part, middle-class. Speaking to Adventists about their church growth in North America, Carl George says, "Your reports show Adventist growth going up year-by-year, but studying those reports carefully shows that your best growth is not occurring in the Anglo world, but in the third world minorities in the U.S. I don't see anything wrong with that at all. I think it is wonderful that you are extending the gospel beyond the Anglo parts of society." [79]

With regard to the issue of communalism, however, Carl George identifies the problems that will prevent additional appropriate growth for Adventists: "Nor should this plateauing of Anglo growth be viewed as a failure for the church. The white populations of North America have changed. Anglos, who showed the greatest potential for Adventist growth until 40 or 50 years ago, no longer present a recruitable target, at least by your current methodologies. Part of this can be attributed to lifestyle changes in America. Part can be attributed to the fact you segregate your children in Adventist schools, diminishing your contact with Gentiles." [80]

At a time when our Anglo church growth has virtually halted in North America, Adventists continue to "communalize" to their own peril. Furthermore, even if it were successful, "communalism" is not biblical. Stott correctly points out that the place for the converted individual is back in the world. "Conversion must not take the convert out of the world but rather send him back into it, the same person in the same world, and yet a new person with new convictions and new standards." [81] That is discipleship.

Our sense of mission and our self-image as faithful remnant drive us to evangelize the world with a last-day message aimed at "preparing a people ready to meet the Lord." Therefore, accurate understanding of prophecy, careful delineation of doctrine, and specific application of standards have been essential in the process of instructing new believers. The quantity versus quality debate has thus been fueled by those who believe insufficient preparation has preceded baptism. Naturally those members or clergy concerned about "numbers" as the only objective of evangelism would stress the need for less quantity and more quality, which they believe is definitely lacking. As noted, Adventists' own remnant concept has contributed to this debate.

> Conversion must not take the convert out of the world, but rather send him back into it.

While there is biblical basis for a remnant theology—God's faithful followers in an age of overwhelming secularism and evil—this view must never be used to justify lack of growth. The danger of the remnant view directed toward lack of growth is not only that it might excuse little growth, it actually might glorify it. Regarding this, McGavran says, "Remnant theology proves attractive. A glorification of littleness prevails, in which to be small is to be holy. Slow growth is adjudged good growth." [82] He points out that slogans and concepts such as the following give false support to this type of remnant theology:

1. The tiny minority suffering for its belief is the true Church.

2. To create this minority is the highest success known to missions.

3. The persecuted Church, the Church under the cross, is the true Church.

4. The power of a small group of men, with God, must never be underestimated.

5. The creative minority is what the Church must ever strive to be." [83]

In general Adventists would reject the "remnant" theology which stresses smallness in favor of a view of a triumphant remnant. On the other hand, we might embrace an equally dangerous "remnant" theology of exclusivity or superiority based on a *knowledge* of "truth." We want our

> Many professing believers remain woefully ignorant about basic facts of Christianity.

new members to be on the "inside" of this "truth track." Typically we expect all new believers to have been instructed thoroughly in all points of doctrine—27 fundamental points, to be exact. Furthermore, we typically expect not only that the information has been conveyed and comprehended, we also want it to be operative within the behavior of the new member prior to baptism.

There is nothing wrong with adequate instruction or thorough preparation of candidates for church membership. The perils of a casual acknowledgment of the gospel without a corresponding impact on the life of the believer are so abundantly visible in our denomination, and others as well, that no serious challenge could be sustained which called for less thorough biblical instruction for new believers. In fact, just the opposite is needed. Jo Lewis and Gordon Palmer demonstrate that "core" spiritual knowledge is lacking in the American society that prides itself on being "Christian"! They cite a 1988 Gallup poll that found many professing believers remain woefully ignorant about basic facts of Christianity. For example, Gallup's study revealed that 85 percent of Americans assent to the validity of the Ten Commandments and believe that someday all will have to answer to God for how they have obeyed or disobeyed them. Unbelievably, however, these same people don't know what the Ten Commandments are. Only a few can name as many as five and, of course, even fewer obey them. Worst of all, Gallup found that evangelical Christians are little better than the general populace. [84] "Young people today know Genesis as the name of a rock band or a planetary project in a *Star Trek* film, but not as the first book of the Bible. They know Pepsi and the new generation, but not heaven and the everlasting generation; *L. A. Law,* but not God's law. They know who makes *180 Z's,* but not the Alpha and Omega who made them. They know Nikes and the winning team, but not victory in Jesus. They know how to look at *Days of Our Lives,* but not how to look into the days of their lives." [85]

Beyond information to lifestyle

Information alone is not the key, however. We need instruction, but we need more instruction in righteousness. We need more thorough spiritual as well as intellectual indoctrination of new believers. This is one of the ingredients of discipleship—perhaps the most basic. "Church growth refers not merely to an outer measurable expansion, but also to an inner experience within the body of Christ. 'But grow in the grace and knowledge of our Lord and Saviour Jesus Christ' " (2 Pet. 3:18).[86] Bellah says, "More than anything else, this generation needs biblical teaching. Our minds need to be renewed with expectations born not in the culture, but in the Word of God . . . Baby boomers need to know that all truth is not relative, and experience is only one test of truth—often misleading in the short run." [87]

Far too often we assume that because something has been stated well, it has been thoroughly comprehended. Michael Green describes the instruction of new members through preaching to be more than just proclaiming truth. It must take root in the heart and be lived out in the life. "We tried to do this (overall church training) in a variety of ways. One was by having carefully planned courses of sermons: sometimes topical, sometimes following the church's year, sometimes expository. We tried to be sensitive to what the needs were at the time. Gradually we learned how foolish we were to dart from subject to subject each week. We needed to go on teaching on a particular topic until it is learned and acted upon. With this in mind, we organized a nine-month course, examining what it meant to be an alternative society in a world that is falling apart. We spent a whole month on each of nine aspects of this theme, and teaching took place at all levels in the church. The team preached on each topic for a whole month. The fellowship groups and prayer meetings discussed its application. Slide-tape sequences were produced for each topic. And we even made a loose-leaf guide book to the whole nine-month series, with opportunities for members to add materials of their own." [88]

Speaking specifically to grounding new believers into the Seventh-day Adventist church, Ellen White admonishes, "If those who knew the truth and were established in it were indeed in need of having its importance kept ever before them and their minds stirred up by the repetition of it, how important that this work is not neglected for those newly come to the faith." [89]

However, a reliance on knowledge alone—conveying correct information into the comprehension of the new believer—may contribute to the Adventist church remaining a closed community more than we have realized. If we conclude that information alone disciples individuals, then we are in danger of spiritual haughtiness similar to that of the Corinthians who concluded that superior wisdom equaled superior spirituality.

I have known dozens of individuals within the Adventist church whose theological comprehension was accurate but whose lives did not reflect the life-changing differences the gospel brings about. Clearly something was needed beyond accurate theology. They needed not only a knowledge of "the truth," they needed a personal relationship with Jesus Christ— "THE Truth"! As Dudley and Cummings say, "If we have nothing more than textual proofs for our distinctive beliefs, we will not begin to earn a hearing, for the world wants to know what meaning and relevance our message has for their lives." [90]

John Stott puts it well: "In addition to integrity, our preaching of repentance and of Christ's lordship requires realism. It is not enough to call people to repentance in vague terms, as if conversion could take place in a kind of mystical vacuum out of which all real life has been sucked. When John the Baptist preached his baptism of repentance he insisted that people responding must 'bear fruits that befit repentance.' Nor did he leave it there. He went on to specific issues. The affluent must share their surplus wealth with the deprived. Tax collectors must replace extortion by probity. And soldiers must never use their power to rob people, but rather be content with their wages (Luke 3:8, 10-14) . . . We need to spell out in realistic and concrete terms the contemporary implications of repentance, conversion, and the lordship of Jesus Christ." [91]

So what is the role of instruction for new converts and its relationship to assimilating the new believers into the life of the church? We have already noted that if instruction produces isolationism or feelings of superiority, it has failed in its objective. Nevertheless, instruction is necessary. In fact, it is vital and foundational. Jesus' commission commands His followers to make disciples, to baptize, and to teach all things that He has commanded (Matt. 28:19-20). The obvious question is when and where that teaching occurs. Ellen G. White says, "After the first efforts have been made in a place by giving a course of lectures, there is really greater necessity for a second course than for the first. The truth is new and startling, and the people need to have the same presented the second time, to get the points distinct and the ideas fixed in the mind." [92]

Michael Green's research points out that in the early days of Christianity, baptism was administered straight away on profession of faith and repentance and that this practice continued at least throughout the first century. "However, the *Didache* suggests that very soon a period of instruction in the Christian faith, particularly its ethical side, preceded baptism," and "It would not be surprising if the early missionaries did soon evolve a stylized form of Christian instruction just as they seem to have done, at least to some extent, with their gospel preaching." [93]

This instruction which accompanied the preaching of the first Christian missionaries seems to have concentrated on four basic areas characterized by four Latin words:

"1. *Deponentes*–The putting off of the old evil nature.

"2. *Subjecti*–Proper Christian submission in various areas of political and social life.

"3. *Vigilate*–The charge to watch and pray.

"4. *Resistite*–The need for standing firm in the faith and for resisting the assaults of the devil." [94]

Green's additional comment on this indoctrinational process of the early church comes directly to the crux of the issue for Adventists. He says, "Whether it [this indoctrinational instruction] preceded baptism or followed it is more problematical." [95] Adventist evangelism has followed a similar process of providing baptismal preparation instruction along with gospel proclamation. For example, a new member in Marietta once observed, "your evangelistic series is, in reality, an enquirer's class." In fact, the very issue of how much of that instruction is pre-baptism and how much should be provided as the newly baptized believer grows has been a vigorously debated topic for at least a generation.

While it is accurate to say, as I have stated earlier, that the church essentially wants all instruction to precede baptism, this has brought its own inherent problems to the process of assimilating new members. The greatest of these problems may be the ability of the new believer to grasp everything in a relatively short period of indoctrination. However, in considering the whole process, the most dangerous of these problems may well be the erroneous conclusion that since converts are so thoroughly indoctrinated prior to baptism, they need no additional or further post-baptismal instruction.

However, Jesus' own words (Matt. 28:19-20) anticipate an instruction that comes after baptism as well as that which is necessary to baptize the convert. The words "teaching them to observe all things" do not precede the experience of baptism in the gospel commission and, for all practical purposes, cannot in the actual life of the new believer. To me, this is theologically persuasive with a definite practical application. If baptism brings a spiritual rebirth (John 3), and if spiritual things are spiritually discerned (1 Cor. 2:14), then some portion of the "all things" that Jesus has commanded cannot be discerned until the individual is spiritually reborn. To attempt to do otherwise is to ignore the process envisioned by the gospel commission.

The content of instruction is important as well. It should be geared both to the level of comprehension and to the level of commitment of the new believer.

The essential and the additional

Further, there should be a core understanding and consensus by the body as to what is essential and what is additional. Herb Miller says, "Trying to get people to 'have the mind of Christ' on moral matters is admirable. But we must always be wary that we are not really trying to get them to 'have our mind' on the matter instead of His. Many who think they are witnessing to God's word are really trying to speak God's word for Him. That subtle form of idol worship tries to take over God's job of being God. 'Accept among you the man who is weak in the faith, but do not argue with him about his personal opinions' (Rom. 14:1) is still excellent advice. Pride in our own righteousness has no place in *word* communication." [96]

How much and what type of instruction is to precede baptism? Peter Wagner addresses this issue in an excellent chapter, *The Gospel, Conversion, and Ethical Awareness.* He says, "There is some risk in keeping the ethical content of discipling to a minimum in preaching free grace. But to me there seems a greater risk in prematurely trying to uproot the tares and destroying some of the wheat in the process. I know of many evangelists who do not insist, as a prerequisite to salvation, that unbelievers agree to tithe their income. But after they become Christians they learn that their new Lord expects them to tithe their income. This is not bothersome to the average Christian. Initial repentance and conversion means turning to 'Christ as the Lord of life, and when, over a lifetime of discipleship, the Lord speaks and brings new requirements to their attention, they are cordially accepted. Taking the step of tithing is an advance in Christian obedience, more a part of perfecting than of discipling.' " [97]

> ∼
> ─────────────
> High secular and cultural attainments must not be mistaken for dedication to Christ.
> ─────────────
> ∼

This "perfecting" role is the privilege and duty of the church. Referring back to McGavran's D-1, D-2, and D-3 definitions of discipleship, the church's mission cannot stop at D-2; it must move forward to D-3, and this must be evidenced in spiritual growth, not just cultural advancement or socioeconomic upward mobility. "A perfecting which lifts educational attainments, increases earning ability, heightens conscience as to social justice, and decreases concern to win kindred to eternal life, betrays the Gospel. High secular and cultural attainments must not be mistaken for dedication to Christ." [98]

When does this D-3 perfecting role occur in the life of the new believer?

"Undisciplined pagan multitudes must be 'added to the Lord' before they can be perfected. The church exists not for herself but for the world. She has been saved in order to save others. She always has a twofold task: winning men to Christ and growing in grace. While these tasks overlap, they are distinct." [99] Obviously the church cannot "teach eggs to fly that have not been hatched." There is an "instruction in righteousness" that is necessary post-baptism as surely as there are essentials that need to be accepted and believed prior to baptism. George Hunter offers these conclusions from a study of about four thousand converts in India: "Their postbaptismal training was more influential in whether they remained and grew in the Christian community than even the motives which originally attracted them to Christianity. I am sure that the first few weeks are equally important to the life of a new convert in any American church." [100]

George Gallup observes, "Many Americans belong to the not quite Christian category: They believe, but without strong convictions. They want the fruits or reward of faith, but seem to dodge the responsibilities and obligations. They say that they are Christian but often without a visible connection to a congregation or religious fellowship. The major challenge appears to be . . . how to guide men and women into becoming mature Christian personalities." [101] Discipleship, then, involves the whole process of initial instruction (prebaptism), welcoming the new member into the community (at baptism for Adventists), and teaching them to observe all things (post-baptism).

And communalism will have its impact. Information may be imperfectly communicated, but in the long run what is "caught" by association with fellow believers may be more important than what is "taught" as far as discipleship is concerned. Richard Neuhaus points this out when he says, "The communal intuition on which they act may not be legitimated by the Christian teaching they hear . . . In that teaching the church may be accidental or even hostile to the process of 'being saved.' But the people, thank God, know better than they are taught. The whole Christian message affirms the majesty of the merely human." [102]

This "teaching" cannot be limited to merely intellectual knowledge. It must be implemented into the life. This is applied theology—applied in the daily Christian walk. Juan Carlos Ortiz points out that this application of discipleship must be conveyed by more than intellectual instruction. "In a discipleship relationship I do not teach the other person to know what I know, rather I teach him to become what I am. Discipleship then is not a communication of knowledge but a communication of life and spirit." [103] Bill Hull says, "The Greek word for disciple–*mathetes*–means learner, pupil, someone who learns by following. The word implies an intellectual process that directly affects the lifestyle of a person." [104]

Growth and faithfulness

Growth and fruitfulness involve a progression of decisions initiated by problem-recognition and followed by a struggle to find the correct application in the life of the believer. If doctrine is imparted devoid of application, it is useless beyond providing mental gymnastics. If Christians aren't receiving solid guidance in applying biblical truth to their daily lives, the church is failing.[105]

> In discipleship I do not teach the other person to know what I know, rather I teach him to become what I am.

If doctrinal instruction alone is insufficient, what are the essential components of discipleship for new believers? What should the church be teaching and doing? Personally, I am convinced that the content of a strategy is not nearly as important as having a strategy developed by the individual congregation for its own unique situation. This does not mean that content is unimportant, but it does suggest that "the process is the product!"

Suggested strategies range from the simple[106] to the complex. Below are several helpful models for instructing and incorporating new believers. However, for our congregation in Marietta, we enumerated five essential ingredients of discipleship, each vitally necessary for spiritual growth. These are:

Bible Study–Time in the Word. Learning both inductive searching of the Scriptures to hear God's personal message and deductive, didactic instruction from Bible-study guides which will lead new believers through basic Scriptural understandings.

Prayer–Communication with God. Learning to talk to God and to hear from God. Individual prayer, prayer with and for other believers, and corporate prayer in the body of believers. New members also should know that their pastor is praying for them individually.

Fellowship–Interaction with other believers through *celebration* (worship with the entire church family), *congregation* (interaction with a group of believers organized around the leadership of an elder) and *cell* (life with a very small group in which the new believer is nurtured and held accountable).[107]

Witnessing–Sharing with others what God has done in the personal life of the believer. As Elton Trueblood says, "No one is really a Christian at all unless he is an evangelist or is getting ready to be one." [108] It is essential to affirm that witnessing is not instructional teaching or correcting erroneous theological beliefs. Rather, witnessing consists of sharing "what wonderful things God has done" in the new believer's life (Mark 5).

Obedience–Applying intellectual understandings into daily life. Incorporating the commands of Christ into "life commandments" that are lived out in the believer's total environment. This obedience is not salvation by works, but a fulfilling of Christ's injunction, "If you love me, keep my commandments" (John 14:15). These good works are the result (fruit) of salvation rather than the way to salvation (Eph. 2:8-10).

The disciplines of Bible study and prayer are directly related to this issue of instruction for new believers since most new converts need to be instructed in how to study the Scriptures and how to pray.[109] This instruction enables believers to articulate their beliefs. The experience of fellowship will be more thoroughly expanded in Chapter 5, which deals with the need for new believers to belong to a group of caring and nurturing friends as the second of these three important strategies.

Chapter 6 will further develop the importance of witnessing and obedience. Witnessing involves the believers in meaningful ministry activities. Jesus' instruction to the delivered demoniac (Mark 5) was not to seek deeper theological understanding or even to isolate himself and pray. His first act of obedience was to "go and tell his friends what wonderful things God had done for him." We need believers who will personally obey what they learn from Bible study, but we must recognize that obedience begins by telling others what God has done.

Resources

Other helpful models of assisting new believers in becoming able to articulate their beliefs and incorporating them into the life of the church can be found by studying the available resources. Some of the most helpful ones are:

The Master's Plan for Making Disciples. An excellent training package by Win and Charles Arn including a textbook, video, and group discussion/implementation items. An example of their practical methods is a six-step outline for making strategy become reality for the church:

1. Build an "incorporation consciousness."
2. Develop an incorporation structure.
3. Provide friendship-building opportunities.
4. Structure need-meeting ministries.
5. Create new roles and tasks.
6. Monitor incorporation results.[110]

The Psychology of Witnessing. A balanced and thoughtful approach to witnessing by psychologist Jard DeVille in which he establishes the premise that believers must earn the right to witness by: (a) Relating in love and support to the individual to whom they wish to witness; (b) Recognizing an individual's needs as he/she sees them; and (c) Recommending a solution that makes sense *to that individual.* DeVille further states that believers only earn the right to recommend a solution after they are certain that they have fulfilled steps "a" and "b." With regard to incorporating the new believer, he outlines three helpful processes of life that can be directly applied in this area: "Learning to Learn, Learning to Choose, Learning to Relate." [111]

Called and Committed: World-Changing Discipleship. David Watson's helpful resource provides a breakdown in every chapter of practical functions of discipleship which grow out of a carefully constructed theological basis. Particularly helpful are chapters 4 *(Called to Making Disciples)*, and 10 *(Discipleship and Simple Lifestyle)*, which deals with obedience. [112]

The Master Plan of Discipleship. Robert Coleman's companion book to his classic, *The Master Plan of Evangelism,* uses the book of Acts as the basis for demonstrating that the basic thrust of Jesus' great commission is as valid today as when it was first given to the disciples. Although specific implementations may change with the times, the New Testament principles for evangelism and discipleship are still valid and necessary today. Coleman's chapter titles alone provide a helpful overview of this resource, and the content of these chapters provides excellent "starter" for a helpful sermon series on the subject of discipleship rooted in the early church's experience as recorded in Acts.

> New Testament principles for evangelism and discipleship are still valid and necessary today.

Disciplemakers' Handbook. Alice Fryling systematizes what it means to nurture a new believer. She outlines what the disciplers should expect to experience, the value of their role for the new believer, and what the disciplers might expect in the life of the convert. This is a practical "how-to" instruction for the individual church member who wishes to become a discipler of new believers. Its best assistance is making the complex seem simple and the awesome appear attainable. [113]

Strategies for Church Growth. Peter Wagner offers strategies for a complete range of evangelistic activities, with particular help in understanding new member assimilation as process by expanding the evangelistic process beyond P-1 (Presence evangelism), P-2 (Proclamation evangelism, and P-3 (Persuasion evangelism). Wagner does this by expanding evangelism into eight "P" functions that are to be viewed in a circular (or cyclical) fashion rather than a linear one. This expansion clarifies the potential for misunderstanding that evangelism stops at the point of decision. Of course, this misunderstanding comes primarily from the inadequacy of the word

> Spiritual rebirth
> is much more
> a process
> than an event.

"persuasion" to convey the entire intent of bringing the new believer beyond decision into responsible service within the fellowship of the church, which Wagner is always ready to point out as the ultimate objective of evangelism. Wagner's eight elements are: Prayer, Planning, Power, Presence (P-1), Proclamation (P-2), Persuasion (P-3), Propagation, and Pedagogy, with the cycle beginning again at prayer.[114]

Welcome to the Family. This resource, prepared by Home Study International of the Adventist Church, offers an excellent introduction to church history, traditions, and subcultural terminology.[115] This book/study course's weakness is most evident by noting that its panel of eight authors and editors are primarily educators and includes no pastors or evangelists who are actually "doing" assimilation. Thus the approach is essentially pedagogical, with the implication that information, alone, will sufficiently integrate the new member into the life of the church. The intent is far better than the finished product, although the information is accurate and user-friendly. The approach, however, is primarily that of conveying factual data.

Welcome! Ervin R. Stutzman[116] has compiled a guide for receiving new members into the church which offers a variety of strategies from the very beginning of the process of attracting potential members (emphasizing truth in advertising and presence evangelism) through to integration into the life of the church (traditions) and moving into service (enlistment for ministry). This book offers helpful biblical insights and practical "how-to" ideas that allow the local congregation to select those that will best fit its own situation.

Chapter 5

Meaningful Relationships for Body Life

A mother was surprised at her little boy's answer about how he liked his first day of school. "I hated it," he said. "They put me in a room full of kids all by myself." Suddenly this new scholar had discovered that he could be lonely in a crowd. Those who join a church in which they do not participate soon feel that they have entered a lonely crowd. "Sitting on the bleachers is fine at ball games. At church, it is deadly. Christians who do not participate either vegetate or evacuate." [117]

A new member without a friend is a tragedy. A new member without a friend becomes a statistical number. Members without a friend are, far too often, a reality in Seventh-day Adventist churches. While the tragedy of new members without friends is a concern for any denomination, Adventists have a greater challenge than most others because of unique factors surrounding the doctrinal instruction that is presented to potential members.

Typical recruitment of new members by Adventist evangelism has emphasized the unique theological positions of the church in comparison with "others" who either lack "full truth" or are unwilling to follow what they know. Thus, Adventists regularly experience an observable phenomenon—the theologically convicted individual who embraces the doctrinal positions of the church and joins a local congregation on the basis of theological convictions alone. These individuals may become members without any interactive acquaintance, much less friendship, between themselves and other members.

While theological convictions are necessary and motivating, beliefs alone are insufficient to keep new members bonded to their new congregation. Thus without sociological factors of friendship and involvement included in their experience, new believers may quickly exit that fellowship which they willingly joined. Because the high level of confidence in the "truthfulness" of Adventist doctrine has not been matched with a high level of fellowship and involvement, expectations have been dashed and new believers may well experience rejection, pain, and anger at the very moment they need love, acceptance, and forgiveness.

When they experience this pain, "members cut themselves off from really committing themselves to one another; they draw back from costly shared life together. It is easier just to go to Sunday morning service . . . or not to go at all. Both amputated limbs and the remaining trunk lose out." [118]

John Savage, Methodist pastor and president of LEAD Consultants, interviewed a group of inactive members regarding their reasons for leaving the church. He says, "Each of the 23 persons interviewed in the non-active group indicated that no one from the church had ever come to find out why they were losing interest or had dropped out. It reinforced their belief that no one cared, and that they were not missed. One third of this group cried during the interview, indicating the intensity of unresolved feelings." [119]

Because these new members believe that they are unwanted and unneeded, it becomes easier for them to develop an attitude of indifference rather than risk rejection. Ken Abraham says: "Most psychologists agree that the opposite of love is not hate; it's indifference. For example, a couple having marital problems has a better chance of reconciliation if there are feelings between them, regardless how negative or bitter those feelings are. But if the couple is indifferent in their feelings, it will take serious, long-term work to recapture the love they once knew . . . The same is true spiritually. Indifference is a killer. Even negative reactions are better then no reaction. If you sense yourself sliding toward spiritual indifference, you must take radical corrective action immediately!" [120]

However, rather than recognizing their own acts of abandonment or the resulting reaction of indifference by the new members, longer-term members, seeking explanation for why new members have left, conclude that the new member's process of indoctrination was insufficient and that this is the cause of their apostasy. Rather than grapple with the reality of the isolation which the new member has experienced, their exit is explained away as "someone who just couldn't stick." Furthermore, those pastors or members whose energies are directed to ongoing recruitment of new members are labeled as interested only in "numbers."

The issue of numbers

Perhaps this is an appropriate time to deal with this issue of "numbers." Pastors with "church growth eyes" [121] in general and Adventist growth pastors and evangelists in particular, risk being accused as interested only in numbers. So what about this so-called "numbers game"? Peter Wagner describes an encounter with an individual who declared his disgust against numbers, "My Bible tells me to *feed* the sheep, not to *count* them!" Wagner describes how he later read Philip Keller's book *A Shepherd Looks at Psalm 23* on this very issue. Keller, a professional sheep rancher says it is "essential for a careful shepherd to look over his flock every day, counting them to see that all are able to be up and on their feet." Wagner then points out, "I believe that counting sheep is such a natural part of the shepherd's life that Jesus took for granted His followers would know that. It is biblical to feed the sheep, but also to count them." [122] In fact, the only way that the Good Shepherd knew that He had one lost sheep was because He had counted the other ninety-nine.

> It is biblical
> to feed the sheep,
> but also
> to count them.

Wagner says, "God Himself does a lot of counting. He even has the hairs on each person's head numbered. When each individual comes to faith in Jesus Christ, that name is written in the Lamb's book of life. Even the littlest person is important in heaven and gets individual recognition. There is joy in heaven over *one* sinner who repents (Luke 15:7), so somebody there must be keeping close track. As I see it, those who object to numbers are usually trying to avoid superficiality in Christian commitment. I agree with this . . . I am not interested in Christians who profess faith in Christ but do not demonstrate it in their lives. These numbers are unimportant. But I am vitally interested in lost men and women who put their faith in Jesus Christ and are born again. I am interested in true disciples who take up their cross daily to follow Jesus. I am interested in kingdom people who relate to Jesus as their Lord. I am interested in Spirit-filled people who have experienced the power of the Holy Spirit and are using their spiritual gifts. I am interested in responsible church members who continue 'steadfastly in the apostles' doctrine and fellowship, in breaking of bread, and in prayers' (Acts 2:42) as did believers in the Jerusalem church. When numbers represent these kinds of people, they are much more than a 'numbers game.' They become a game of life and death, a game of time or eternity. The stakes are the highest in the world, for 'he who has the Son has life; he who does not have the Son of God does not have life' (1 John 5:12)." [123]

When Jesus commanded His disciples to go into all the world and make disciples of all nations, He was concerned about numbers—numbers of persons who would become disciples. To those who criticize that we ought to be really concerned with just one or a few, not the numerous mass of humanity, Bailey E. Smith has given an appropriate response: "Let's never forget that numbers are all multiples of one. One hundred is a hundred ones; a thousand, a thousand ones; so it is possible to be honestly concerned about each one of several thousand ones. We need concern for all!" [124]

The Great Commission is included in each of the four gospels as well as the book of Acts (Matt. 28:19-20; Mark 16:15; Luke 24:46-49; John 20:21; Acts 1:8). Clearly Christ's mandate is that His church should multiply, not simply maintain. The book of Acts is the story of the church's rapid growth—and it talks

> ∼
>
> **If the church is interested in what interests Jesus, it will be interested in numbers.**
>
> ∼

about numbers! "Three thousand were baptized at Pentecost" (Acts 2:41). "The Lord added to their number daily" (2:47). "Many who heard the message believed, and the number of men grew to about five thousand" (4:4). "More and more men and women believed in the Lord and were added to their number" (5:14). "The number of disciples in Jerusalem increased rapidly, and a large number of priests became obedient to the faith" (6:7). "It [the church] was strengthened and encouraged by the Holy Spirit, it grew in numbers, living in the fear of the Lord" (9:31). "The Lord's hand was with them, and a great number of people believed and turned to the Lord" (11:21). "So the churches were strengthened in the faith and grew daily in numbers" (16:5).

Nelson Annan says of Acts 2, "I used to focus solely on verse 42, which emphasizes four marks of the New Testament church … but in this passage Luke also mentions numerous conversions and baptisms, generosity and sharing, and gladness and praise (2:41, 43-47). And in this context Luke emphasizes numerical growth *twice*." [125] The message is obvious. If the church is going to be interested in what interests Jesus, it will be interested in numbers—numbers of people for His kingdom!

Friendship with new believers

Of course this brings us right back to the issue of friendship and involvement with new believers. People are no longer numbers when we love them, when we value them, when we pray for and with them, and when we minister to them. Bailey Smith recounts the story of a Sunday school teacher who responded to a criticism of numbers with determination to emphasize quality. Next week he arrived at class to discover several of his youngsters missing. Then his love for them and concern for their souls led him on an all-out effort to get them back to class. He concluded, "Shall we strive for numbers—Yes, O Yes! When it is *my* boys, let's have numbers—all eleven of them!" [126]

Numbers, then, are important only because they represent individuals who need to be reached for Christ. In fact, when we understand numbers from this perspective, we realize that an individual remains only a number until someone becomes his or her friend and takes a personal interest. Making friends becomes not only a much-needed and excellent method of follow-up to assimilate new members, but also an effective evangelistic strategy.

> Before we can win people to Jesus Christ we must win them to ourselves.

R. Paul Stevens observes, "The most important thing we can do, then, toward equipping all the saints for ministry is to shape the environment in unity and complementarity so that every member 'hears' from the environment the message: not *you*, but *we*; not your personal self-development, but building up the body as 'each part does its work.' " [127]

For Adventists, in particular, this is a crucial lesson to learn. If we embrace only one primary evangelistic strategy–prophetic-based gospel proclamation and doctrinal instruction–we face two dangers. We risk limiting those whom we could win and we risk losing those whom we have won! Tom Stebbins says: "Someone has suggested that before we can win people to Jesus Christ we must win them to ourselves. Sharing the gospel is a very personal matter. We are probing the most intimate, private areas of the other person's life so we must first earn that person's trust and build some measure of friendship." [128]

If this is essential in getting decisions, it is equally vital in keeping the converts attached to the body, both in emotional as well as physical proximity.

Furthermore, this evangelistic strategy of friendship is a generationally-relevant issue. Brux Austin, editor-in-chief of *Texas Business*, describes baby boomers as having been programmed to acquire at the expense of both personal integrity and personal fulfillment. "What good is lolling in your Jacuzzi in the beautiful back yard of your breathtaking home if you feel an aching emptiness in your innards—a chronic pain that all the wine coolers in the world can't numb?" [129] Friendship involvement with baby boomers may become the most effective strategy for evangelizing them and group interaction is a proven method for reaching GenXers.

Bruce Larson describes how the neighborhood bar becomes the substitute for the church in meeting the needs of unchurched individuals longing for friends: "It's an imitation, dispensing liquor instead of grace, escape rather than reality, but it is a permissive, accepting, and inclusive fellowship. It is unshockable. It is democratic. You can tell people secrets and they usually don't tell others or even want to. The bar flourishes, not because most people are alcoholics, but because God has put into the human heart the desire to know and be known, to love and be loved, and so many seek a counterfeit at the price of a few beers." [130]

There is an interesting connection between Jerry Cook's model of love, acceptance, and forgiveness and the three points Sharon Cress identifies about articulating belief, having friends, and meaningful involvement that we have utilized as the basis for chapters 4-6.

Jerry Cook says there are three guarantees from the church that people must have before they will risk becoming open enough to receive the healing that brings spiritual maturity and wholeness. First, the guarantee that they will be loved—always, under every circumstance, with no exception. Second, that they will be totally accepted, without reservation. Third, that no matter how miserably they fail or how blatantly they sin, unreserved forgiveness is theirs for the asking.[131] The first and second of these guarantees are crucial in the impact of friendship for new members.

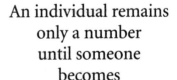

An individual remains only a number until someone becomes his or her friend.

A friend will love a friend and accept that person for who he/she is— warts and all! A friend will seldom do this for a stranger. Strangers will find little acceptance, little love, and virtually no forgiveness from a group of people who do not know them. Further, no matter how theologically persuaded new members are of the doctrinal positions of their new church, without friendship it is nearly impossible to remain in fellowship. When new members are recruited on the basis of doctrine alone, without fellowship as a strong and accompanying reality, we are setting both ourselves and the new member up for failure.

Rather than assuring that new believers either already have friends or gain new friends within the congregation, Adventist church members often adopt a "holier than thou" attitude that excludes people at the very moment

~

We are concerned for our unsaved loved ones. Are we concerned for our unloved saved ones?

~

that they most need inclusion. "They feel the churches have closed their doors against them. A divorcee perceives herself as 'not good enough.' A black janitor sees himself as overlooked, 'the invisible American.' A young sculptor in California analyzes his church experiences. 'Dead people going in,' he says, 'no life in them, sitting in pews, coming out. Rich people sit in the front, poor people sit in the back. Years of that makes you dried up ... They got their own little group, their own little people.' " [132] As Christians we are rightfully concerned for our unsaved loved ones. Perhaps we should show equal concern for our unloved saved ones.[133]

Applying Cook's first step to this issue of "having friends within the church," notice what he says: "Love means accepting people the way they are for Jesus' sake. Jesus hung around with sinners and if we're too holy to allow people to blow smoke in our faces, then we're holier than Jesus was. He didn't isolate Himself in the synagogue. In fact, He mixed with sinners so much that the self-righteous got upset about it. 'He's friendly with some very questionable people,' they said. And Jesus replied, 'Yes, because I didn't come to minister to you religious leaders. I came to call sinners to repentance.' Isn't that fantastic? Jesus spent His time with dirty, filthy, stinking, bent sinners. And when those kind of people find someone who will love and accept them, you won't be able to keep them away!" [134]

This is the very essence of discipling! This is the very process of nurturing new members to the point of fruit-bearing maturity, and the best "first fruit" they can bear will be extending love, acceptance, forgiveness, and friendship with another new believer. "Pastors are not obligated to get people to heaven. That's the work of Jesus. A pastor's obligation to people is first to love and accept and forgive them, and second, to bring them to ministry readiness by teaching them to do the same." [135]

And even this emphasis on extending forgiveness and acceptance relates directly back to the first step of articulating the doctrines–the most essential one being salvation by grace through faith in Christ Jesus. The Adventist church needs continually to relearn that Jesus accepts us though our lives have much that offends His holiness. Righteousness by faith in His merits says that His acceptance of us does not imply approval of our misbehavior, but rather it shows love that will transcend our shortcomings and transform our behavior into His likeness if we will only allow sufficient time to interact with Him as a "friend who sticks closer than a brother"! If we, then, are acceptable to Jesus despite our lack, how could we dare reject others?

We must stop playing God and start experiencing and teaching godlikeness. This is the difference between the world and the church. In God's kingdom we first love, then we move into acquaintance and friendship. In the world, we first get acquainted, then we move into love, sometimes. As a result, most people have many acquaintances and a few friends, perhaps, but are dying from lack of love.[136]

When new believers embrace the church but do not, in return, feel embraced, then their expectations are dashed against harsh rocks of indifference. This is particularly significant when we realize that many people seek the Saviour and embrace the church at a time of change or trauma in their life circumstances. One of the sociological motivations for joining a church–notwithstanding personal commitment to Jesus Christ– is the human need to belong.

Psychologist Maslow's hierarchy of needs demonstrates that once a person moves beyond assuring the essentials to sustain life and safety, the next priority is to "belong." Further, the more change or trauma individuals have experienced, the more likely that their sense of belonging may be damaged or that their need for a new "reference group identification" has become acute. For such people, conversion would establish a new self-defining group affiliation to take the place of identifications which have been broken by changes in their life situations.[137]

> The expectations of new believers become dashed against the hard rocks of indifference.

Kent Hunter, following Wagner's model of *celebration, congregation,* and *cell,* advocates intentionally establishing new fellowship groups as the church grows. He points out several benefits of this intentional structuring of new congregations: "It will enable people to continue to feel a part of the fellowship family, even as the church grows. It will allow the church to grow without major resistance. It will be the setting in which people are tied into the Word of God, and it will help with the assimilation of new members—an important church growth concern."[138]

The probability of new members becoming actively involved in the church is directly tied to the number of friends that they develop soon after joining the church. In his dissertation study, Flavil Yeakley interviewed fifty lay members who had been in the church for six months and were now actively involved (incorporated) in the life of the church as well as fifty recent converts who had joined the church but had since dropped out. He identified the number of friends that each new convert established during the first six months of membership. His findings are interesting. The more quickly new members formed a number of personal relationships within the congregation, the more likely they were to become active and involved. The converts who stayed had developed an average of more than seven new friends in the church. Those who dropped out could identify an average of fewer than two changes in friendship pattern.[139]

Warren Hartman asked two questions of those who had recently dropped out of church: 1) Why they dropped out? and 2) What would most influence their choice of a new church home? The answer regularly given to the first question was "Did not feel part of the group." The response to the second (nearly 75 percent) was "friendliness of the people."[140]

> ~
> ## Friendliness is different from being friend-seeking.
> ~

Members in the churches from which these new members dropped out most likely did not consider themselves unfriendly. New members are not necessarily overtly rejected by those already within the fellowship. Quite often there is a superficial level of friendliness which, like my self-description of "Southern hospitality," is a mile wide and a quarter-inch deep. In fact, most Adventist congregations would be shocked if they were described as unfriendly. Friendliness is different, however, from being friend-seeking. Common courtesy and genteel manners will lead a group of people in a public setting to act in a friendly manner. On the other hand, the real message that may be conveyed is, "Please don't bother me with depth beyond the superficial greeting."

One new member in my former congregation stated, "I get the real impression that when someone asks how I'm doing they really don't want to know and would be shocked if I even attempted to tell them. They are expressing a friendly greeting, but they don't want to be my friend."

Rejection of superficial courtesy in lieu of genuine friendship should not surprise us. As Ken Abraham observed: "The opposite of love is not hate; it's indifference."[141]

With regard to nurturing people into the life of the body of believers, too many of our churches are better in form than in reality. We say the right things, but we don't have the loving, supportive relationship to back up our words. We may think we are friendly while, in fact, guests or new members do not sense a loving atmosphere at all. Nelson Annan suggests a six-step approach toward nurturing friendship-building, inclusive relationships within a congregation:

1. *Communicate love.* Some leaders may be strong in organizing, teaching, and leading committee meetings, but weak when it comes to relating to people. Leaders must not only love the flock, but communicate that love. Loving churches have leaders who effectively communicate their love.

2. *Preach and teach love.* The individual in the pulpit can best challenge the church to grow in love for God, for one another, and for the world around them. This is the leader's privilege and responsibility.

3. *Emphasize friendliness and warmth.* People-oriented greeters who smile, love to talk, and remember names should stand at the door to greet visitors. Name tags help new people learn names. Ushers should be helpful and friendly.

4. *Follow up your visitors.* Cultivate friendships with visitors. In growing congregations a visitor should receive one or more of the following gestures: a lunch invitation; a telephone call expressing pleasure at his/her visit; a letter to encourage a return visit; a personal visit by someone who attempts to build the bridge of friendship and, possibly, to share the gospel.

5. *Broaden the inner groups.* Loving churches make new people feel like they belong. Christians new to the area (potential transfers) should be surrounded with warmth and love. They should be made to feel welcome, and that interest must be genuine or it quickly will be detected as artificial.

6. *Strengthen and increase social events.* In loving churches people spend time together outside of the church building. In order to build relationships, more time is needed than ten minutes before or after meetings. Create unique ways to bring dozens of people together to play and laugh, to work and serve, and to learn and pray together.[142]

In his discussion, *The Dynamics of Inclusion and Exclusion,* Lyle Schaller says that in the typical congregation, most new adult members fall into one of five categories within a year of uniting with the church:

1. Those who become part of a group where membership in that face-to-face group is meaningful *before* formally uniting with the congregation. They are assimilated before they join. An example of this is the man who comes down out of the choir loft in his robe to join other individuals who are making a commitment to membership.

2. Those who become members of a group in which membership is meaningful *after* uniting with the congregation. They gain a sense of acceptance and belonging through membership in that smaller group. Examples of such subgroups include the choir, prayer fellowships, Bible study groups, support groups, functional committees, etc.

3. Those who are assimilated by accepting *a role or office* which gives them a sense of belonging and causes them to identify with the congregation. Examples include a counselor for the youth group, Sunday school teacher, usher, trustee, etc.

4. Those who are assimilated by accepting a *task or job* which has no formal status but which includes specific responsibilities which help the new member gain a sense of acceptance and belonging and to begin to identify with the congregation. These tasks might include helping clean the church, preparing refreshments, counting offerings, making telephone calls, or providing transportation.

5. Those who do not fit into any of these categories. Most of them have dropped out, are in the process of dropping out of the church, or have settled into comparative inactivity.[143]

Embracing the church

If assimilation into the body is the objective, then the demand is for methodology that impacts the life of the new believer. New believers must embrace ownership of the church and its mission at as effective a commitment level as those committed members who have preceded them. They must own the same vision both for the church and for their own relationship to the body of believers. Barna discovered that successful churches incorporate new members into meaningful relationship with the church by passing on their vision of what the church should be. Among the strategies he identifies in these user-friendly churches were:

1. Devoting a significant portion of the new member class to a detailed explanation of the vision.

2. Preaching an annual sermon devoted to restating the vision and tying it to the goals and programs of the church.

3. Placing a statement of the vision in high profile church publications such as the weekly bulletin, newsletter, or other member communication vehicle.

4. Providing an audiotape of the vision, explained by the pastor, to all who were involved in the church.

5. Having every ministry leader (elders, deacons, chairpersons of ministry teams) include with any request for new resources (money, time, labor, materials) a justification based upon the meshing of the activity with the vision.[144]

The principle remains. New members must have something more than head knowledge regarding what they believe. Meaningful relationships and ministry tasks are not only the fruit of a disciplined individual, but are also the methodology for accomplishing that discipleship. These relationships and tasks are the process! This process is the product!

Chapter 6

New Jobs for New Members

God's original plan for humanity included meaningful work. In Eden, His intention for human happiness included employing the capabilities that He had bestowed upon His creatures. "God said to them, Be fruitful and multiply; fill the earth and subdue it; have dominion over the fish of the sea, over the birds of the air, and over every living thing that moves on the earth" (Gen.1:28). "Then the Lord God took the man and put him in the garden of Eden to tend and keep it" (Gen. 2:15).

Adventists, who affirm the importance of the fourth commandment's injunction to "rest" on the seventh day (Ex. 20:8-11), need to remember that the same commandment enjoins working the other six days. Indolence is as much disobedience as irreverence.

So it is with unused spiritual gifts. The New Testament tells us, "But to each one of us grace was given according to the measure of Christ's gift. Therefore He says: When He ascended on high, He led captivity captive, and gave gifts to men" (Eph. 4:7-8). To the extent church members refuse to employ their spiritual gifts in service to the Saviour, to that extent they disobey our Lord's intention. To the extent we allow the spiritual gifts of new members to remain undiscovered or underemployed in service to the Saviour, to that extent we propagate disobedience and encourage spiritual poverty.

"Many of us do not realize how important it is to serve others. The Holy Spirit equips us to minister. If we do not give it away, we get spiritually puffy" says Robert Tuttle.[145] E. Glenn Hinson adds: "In spite of its affirmation of the priesthood of all believers, there is perhaps no function which Protestantism has so much neglected. Not only have Protestant laymen not assumed the priestly role, but until recently even the clergy have shunned it. A major task for Protestant churches today, not merely the clergy, but the whole church, is to understand and accept their priesthood."[146]

The need for the church at large—and the Adventist church in particular—is to remember that the call to salvation is a call to discipleship. That means a call to active ministry by every believer. A believer who is not ministering is, essentially, not a believer. No excuse is sufficient. Examples abound of infirm, housebound individuals who have used letters and telephone calls to serve others effectively. "There is no such thing as being a member of the church without also being a 'minister' and a 'missionary'. . . Essentially, the layman and the clergyman do not belong to different categories . . . The layman has no less responsibility for fulfilling his ministry than has the pastor." [147]

During the days of Oliver Cromwell, England faced a serious financial crisis. Attempting to solve the problem, Cromwell and his financial advisers thought of the gold and silver statues of the saints in the churches throughout the land. The call went out, "Melt down the saints and put them into circulation." [148] This is what the church needs today—putting the saints into circulation!

R. C. Halverson says: "The authentic impact of Jesus Christ in the world is the collective influence of individual Christians right where they are, day in, day out. Doctors, lawyers, merchants, farmers, teachers, accountants, laborers, students, politicians, athletes, clerks, executives . . . quietly, steadily, continually, consistently infecting the world where they live with a contagious witness of the contemporary Christ and His relevance to life." [149]

Christian influence and ministry

This issue of Christian influence and ministry particularly impacts what we do with new believers. Just as the first learning patterns of children will govern their future behavior, so the first learning patterns of baby Christians will determine their future discipleship. John Wesley insisted that to lead people to Jesus Christ without also providing an adequate opportunity for growth and nurture is simply "to beget children for the murderer." [150] Tuttle adds: "I am personally convinced that the only way to keep Christians alive is to keep them moving. The Christian walk is much like riding a bicycle; we are either moving forward or falling off." [151] Thus, it is the church's responsibility not only to ensure that each new believer is taught to *ride* the bicycle, but to ensure that the new believer gets on-going exercise and stays on the path. This cannot be done without helping new believers discover and employ their spiritual gifts.

Typically we have considered the first ministry of new believers to nonbelievers to be that of direct witnessing, and there is certainly biblical support for such a concept. When the demoniac of Gadera was healed (Mark 5), Jesus did not yield to the man's begging to join His group of disciples, but instead sent him back to his own village. "Go home to your friends, and tell them what great things the Lord has done for you and how He has had compassion on you" (Mark 5:19). Verse 20 tells us that the man's witness was not without results, and when Jesus later returned to that region, there were believers there, apparently a result of the man's ministry.

However, while witnessing to others should be one desirable result of coming to Jesus, evangelism is not the only gift of the Holy Spirit. New believers should be led to discover that which best fits their own capabilities and Spirit-given gifts. Otherwise, witnessing may be the result of a religious compulsion or the new believer's guilty regret for "wasted" years. If new believers are "forced" into one mold of ministry, they may

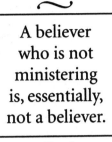

A believer who is not ministering is, essentially, not a believer.

become frustrated and potential souls may be lost to Christ's kingdom.

Believers may be categorized into five witnessing types:

1. The strong, silent type. Says he/she just lives his/her faith.

2. Happens to drop the fact that he/she has been to church or says his/her prayers.

3. The "won't you attend?" type. Invites people to a service to hear someone else say what he/she does not have the courage to personally say.

4. The public-speaking type. Speaks forthrightly in classes, meetings, or services in a way he/she is not quite able to do individually.

5. The conversational/relational type. Witnessing derives from a relationship with Jesus and flows naturally in and through the person's conversation and daily activities.[152]

"Much modern exhortation to witness is futile and may actually be harmful. If men do not have a vital up-to-date relationship with Christ, witnessing can become pharisaical religious proselytizing so we can hang up more scalps on our ecclesiastical belts or pad our religious pride by the number of visits we made . . . A failure to engage in some high-pressure witnessing activity may pile up layers of religious guilt for not witnessing. Consequently, when we do speak to others for Christ, it is out of fear and guilt more than out of faith and guidance. The result? Not much! Compulsive witnessing may have the thrasher going wide open, but not much wheat comes out."

Witnessing, then, is not something we "do" as much as something we "are." A relationship with Jesus produces the fruit of Christian character, and this, unconsciously, even more than consciously on our part, draws men to Christ. Jesus told His disciples, "Ye shall receive power, after that the Holy Spirit is come upon you; and ye shall be witnesses unto me" (Acts 1:8). "Christ says that Christian witnessing is not optional. But neither is it mandatory. It is inevitable." [153]

> ~
> ### Witnessing is not something we "do" as much as something we "are".
> ~

Employment of spiritual gifts in ministry is important for spiritual growth in the life of the new believer, and its vital role should not be underestimated. McGavran and Arn say, "Inherent in being saved was that the redeemed share the good news." [154] However, while the Spirit's purpose in bestowing gifts is two-fold—increasing the kingdom as well as increasing the faith of the new believer—we should not confuse *ministry,* in which every believer must engage, with *evangelism,* which is one of many gifts the Holy Spirit gives.

This is a subtle, but important, distinction. The *ministry* of every believer provides a witness, but every life of *witness* has not been given the gift of evangelism. We must carefully maintain this distinction in order to assist new believers, first, not to feel frustrated if their spiritual gift is not evangelism and, second, to encourage them to discover and utilize that which the Spirit has given them in *ministry.* In her little book, *Beyond Baptism,* an introduction to what new believers should know about the Adventist lifestyle, Fannie Houck says, "It is important that the new believer 'settle in' to the Christian way of life quickly and solidly. This process, called discipling, includes learning how to gain spiritual victory, how to prioritize and use personal resources in God's service, and *how to work effectively* for Him." [155]

Therefore, our need is to employ the energy and enthusiasm of new believers in such a way that it builds their own spiritual strength and thus nurtures their own relationship with their Saviour and, simultaneously, accomplishes ministry for the kingdom. Stott says, "If Jesus' first command was 'come!', His second was 'go!', that is, we are to go back into the world out of which we have come, and go back as Christ's ambassadors." He quotes the report, *The Church for Others:* "The biblical view of conversion envisages a double movement, the turning away from preoccupation with one's own interest and the turning towards the interests of the neighbor (Philippians 2:3). It is a movement of turning away from the world in that the terms of the world, based on self-interest, can no longer be accepted. At the same time, it is a turning *towards* the world, now seen from the perspective of hope in the light of God's purpose." [156]

Unfortunately, studies show that even among believers the concept of turning toward the world in ministry is diminishing to the point that it soon may become extinct. In surveys that back his report, *What Americans Believe*, George Barna discovered that there is not one demographic group of believers in which adult members are spending more time in church-related activities (much less ministry activities) than they were one year ago. He says, "The bad news for churches is that across-the-board people are spending less time participating in church activities. On the other hand, 26 percent report they are spending more time watching television and 55 percent report watching about the

> Inherent
> in being saved
> is that the redeemed
> share
> the good news.

same amount as they did one year ago. Furthermore, although sociological studies demonstrate Americans to be among the loneliest people on earth, you might expect people to spend increasing amounts of time with friends. Sadly, just the opposite is happening. There is actually a net decrease, albeit small, in the proportion of adults who are spending more time with friends than they did one year ago. Isolationism is becoming a way of life in virtually every area. The potential negative impact of this upon the ministry of the church is staggering." [157]

It is the privilege and responsibility of the church to see that new believers are taught to minister. In fact, we will be judged, both corporately and individually, for squandered resources that could and should have been utilized in ministry for the Saviour. Oscar Thompson says, "Someday all Christians will give an account of their lives to the Lord. He has given us many commandments by which we are to live. His last commandment, often called the Great Commission, is found in Matthew 28:19-20. . . . In our concentric circles, everyone has a Jerusalem, a Judea, a Samaria, and a world. Jesus said to start where you are and move forward. Where are you now? Where are you going? Jesus told us to make disciples. Are you?" [158]

New members and their "extended family"

Win and Charles Arn point out that involving new members in witnessing activities is not an optional, but an essential part of the process of effective disciple making. They point out that some of the most receptive people to the gospel are the "extended family" members of new believers—friends, relatives, and associates who are outside of Christ and a church. The Arns have also developed a six-step process for introducing these "extended family" members to Christ by teaching new converts to relate to their extended families by:

1. *Caring.* Personifying Christ's love. Attempting to meet the felt needs of those with whom the new believer has an acquaintance relationship.

2. *Strengthening Relationships.* Table-talk settings in which stronger relationships are built through casual and comfortable interaction.

3. *Involving Other Members of the Body.* Introducing extended family to other believers as a way of introducing them to the wide variety of ways in which Jesus works in the lives of people.

4. *Enhancing Personal Witness.* Using Scripture appropriately to expand the understanding of God's will in various real-life circumstances. This is less than P-2, but more than P-1 evangelism.

5. *Providing a Variety of Exposures.* Special events, public meetings, or gospel presentations which move beyond one-on-one spiritual encounters, but to which the extended family members are brought by the new believer who becomes the catalyst for his/her extended family's increasing involvement with spiritual things.

6. *Developing Patience.* Remembering that each person in the extended family is at a different level of spiritual development. Not all fruit ripens at the same time. Consistency from the new believer toward his/her extended family is more to be desired than quick results.[159]

Expecting and enabling new believers to minister is obedience to our Lord's command and it is a necessary part of the process by which new believers become disciples. McGavran and Hunter, discussing "Training the Laity for Church Growth," argue that all three terms in the title are crucial:

For Church Growth. The training must be for growth, the goal must be clear, and it must be defended against multitudinous good things which obscure it.

> Church growth must be defended against multitudinous good things which obscure it.

The Laity. The laity must be trained. It might start with the clergy, but only as it surges out beyond these professionals and enrolls great numbers of your members will danger be averted.

Training. The process includes motivating, goal setting, instructing, exhorting, building up convictions, harnessing sociological data, practice (actually doing), feedback, and improvement. This is not a quick and easy gimmick. It is a costly venture with the unalterable purpose to seek and save the lost.[160]

Allan Hadidian approaches putting new members to work in ministry from a similar perspective. He says, "Three processes must be used: teaching, training and transforming. Teaching involves knowledge and emphasizes the principles a disciple should know. Training involves skill and emphasizes the practical things a disciple should be able to do. Transforming involves conviction and emphasizes the perspective a disciple should have." [161] Notice the emphasis on "doables." Far too often new members are led to believe that they should be spectators rather than participants. In fact, spiritual strength and maturity will come only as they participate as "co-laborers" with Christ for the lost.

> Far too often
> new members
> are led to believe that
> they should be
> spectators rather
> than participants.

Actions confirm belief. By ministering, new believers live out Jesus' own life of service as He empowers them by the Holy Spirit. To paraphrase Peter Wagner, any scheme that separates ministry action from discipleship has built into itself its own destruction.

Lindgren and Shawchuck call this process of putting new members into ministry "spiritual empowerment." They say, "Our understanding of spiritual empowerment is that it is an ongoing pilgrimage involving an open search for, and sensitivity to experiencing, a growing relationship with God that expresses itself in behavioral action both personally and corporately." [162]

In other words, the process of conversion remains incomplete until new believers are involved in meaningful personal ministry as an integral part of a wider corporate strategy of utilizing the gifts of the Holy Spirit to their fullest potential for the salvation of the lost.

In reality, this is what many people are looking for and longing to receive from the church. They need something more than just a friendly greeting, no matter how genuine or well intentioned such a welcome is. They need and expect involvement. Nelson Annan says, "Some churches welcome people the first Sunday they visit, but no other interaction ever takes place. Newcomers are not challenged to get involved in the church. Eventually they begin attending some other church where they are not only warmly welcomed, but also encouraged to be an active part of the family." [163]

Appropriate balance is the issue. Calling, equipping, and sending must occur simultaneously within the body. While some are being trained, others are being deployed who are calling yet others to decision and discipleship. Dudley and Cummings say: "Church growth must involve all of this. Its insistence on quality balances its concern for quantity. The whole includes proclaiming the gospel, winning and baptizing converts, incorporating them into responsible membership, nurturing their spiritual development, equipping them for further service, motivating them to missionary tasks, and supporting them as they go out to exercise their gifts in bringing in still others. Unless the whole cycle is in place and functioning, the feverish attempt to add to the membership rolls by baptizing will soon break down for lack of a support system." [164]

New members and church renewal

Of course, the constant challenge is to maintain the interest in follow-up activities, without which the interest in outreach activities will surely wane. Ray Sells and Donald LaSuer say, "Some churches are effective in locating and reaching new persons, but as one moves toward nurturing, including assimilating functions, the energy level and effectiveness dramatically declines. The result is many persons whose commitment and faith is aroused but who are never given full opportunity to belong, grow, and serve." [165] Spiritual choices that do not continue on into spiritual service eventually conclude as spiritual disasters.

The impact of new members becoming active in ministry brings benefit for the congregation as well as spiritual growth for the individual. Schaller says, "A flood of new members is the most effective route to church renewal." [166] Of course this brings its own challenges for the church. As Schaller notes: "The larger the flood of new members, the more innovations they introduce, the more influential they are in changing the congregational life-style from passive to active, the greater the impact the new members have on the decision-making processes, the stronger the influence of these new members in redefining the role of that congregation, and the more successful they are in developing new programs—the greater the chances some of the long-time members will feel threatened by the changes." [167]

> The process of conversion remains incomplete until new believers are involved in meaningful personal ministry.

Evangelism is the best place for the newly evangelized individual to minister. Even the fear of potential change on the part of older, more-established members should not deter us from enlisting new converts in direct outreach ministries. Calvin Ratz says, "Established church members may be good people, strong financial supporters of the church's ministries, and even involved in running some of the existing programs of the church. But many are just not into talking about their faith to non-Christians. New converts do. They take to sharing their faith naturally, so we don't want to make the mistake of putting them to work staffing programs that serve the existing church." [168]

In fact, putting new members to work in evangelism is essential for keeping them in the church. In his analysis of user-friendly, growing churches, Barna found a real danger in

> Putting new members to work in evangelism is essential for keeping them in the church.

allowing members to concentrate on themselves in the hope that these individuals might achieve personal wholeness and then feel released to focus on others. He says, "This process is self-defeating if the church allows its people to wait for perfection before concentrating on other people. The churches studied . . . generally taught a divergent path to personal growth. They suggested that the best way to achieve self-growth was by focusing on others, not self. Rather than encouraging people to seek wholeness by making their own interests paramount, they taught the value of ministering to others as a means of ministering to self." [169]

As a matter of fact, it is when all the various individual members of a church are joined in visionary spirit and practical implementation of assigned tasks that the church overcomes the inherent "fear" that new members will take over the church. Common aims shared by the broad group enable boundaries of class, race, gender, and social distinction to be overcome in pursuance of the greater goal.

Speaking of Paul's encouragement to his newly-established churches to collect relief funds for the Jerusalem church, F. F. Bruce says: "It was a common enterprise like this, rather than any formal organization, that first bound the churches together and gave them a sense of unity, or at least enabled them to express their unity . . . This positive bond of unison (surrounding a ministry task) gave cohesion to the Christian groups and to the Christian society as a whole." [170]

Resources

Resources for training new believers and recently transferred members to become effective in ministry are abundant. Some of the easiest to obtain and utilize are indicated below:

The Care and Feeding of Volunteers. [171] Recent studies reveal that 30-65 percent of local church members are willing to serve their respective churches in some sort of volunteer capacity. Douglas Johnson explores the unique motivations, ambitions, and needs of these valuable individuals, emphasizing what makes volunteers want to work and what gives them nonmonetary satisfaction. He discusses how to identify, recruit, and train volunteers and how to enable them to recruit and train other volunteers.

What Can We Do About Church Dropouts?[172] Why do members drop out and what can the church do to slow the stream of dropouts? C. Kirk Hadaway provides helpful and colorful answers as he arranges those who have drifted away, fled, or been pushed out into distinct categories such as Estranged Mental Members, Young Settled Liberals, Young Libertarians, and Irreligious Traditionalists. In addition to describing social characteristics and attitudes of each group, Hadaway demonstrates how to reach these individuals using both innovative and traditional approaches to ministry.

> A well-discipled
> lamb will
> become a
> well-disciplined
> sheep.

Care of Converts.[173] This little book presents itself as a leadership training manual for discipleship with the slogan, "A well-discipled lamb will become a well-disciplined sheep." Perhaps its strongest contribution is its recognition that discipleship of new believers is the responsibility of more people than just the clergy. Keith Bailey says, "New Christians need personal discipleship care. Laymen need to join hands with the pastor in giving this care."[174]

Finding Them, Keeping Them.[175] Gary McIntosh and Glen Martin provide one of the most concise and practical books on this topic. They include specific strategies for both evangelism and assimilation. Their five strategies for assimilation are: Friendship, Task/Roles, Small Groups, Identification, and Spiritual Growth.[176]

30 Days to Understanding the Christian Life.[177] A thorough approach to what God expects of Christians. Particularly helpful are sections 5 and 6. In section 5, Anders discusses Spiritual Warfare: "When we enter the Christian life, we enter not a playground but a battlefield. Life is not a waltz. It's a war. In addition to the snares we might inadvertently step into on our journey, we must be constantly on guard against spiritual attack."[178] In Section 6, he discusses Spiritual Disciplines: "Living the Christian life is like paddling upstream. If you stop making forward motion, you automatically begin traveling backward."[179]

~ Part III ~

Sociological Issues

The axiom is true—the more things change the more they stay the same. The more our congregation attempted to define our uniqueness, the more we discovered we are like those among whom we live and those who are in congregations similar to ours in size and setting of other denominations.

George Barna's description of the changing values of the 90s is an appropriate description of our congregation as our individual members and family units struggled to relate their religious experience to real life and the competing demands for their time, money, energy, and emotional resources. The following chart summarizes Barna's understanding:

Our Changing Values

We used to value:	We are going to value:
Quantity of Possessions	Quality of Possessions
Money	Time
Old Traditions	New Traditions
Commitment	Flexibility
Group Identity	Individualism
Trusting People	Proven Integrity
Satisfaction through Work	Satisfaction through Leisure[180]

Perhaps our greatest challenge is low-level commitment, which Barna says is one of the hallmarks of 90s society. We often described ourselves as a "Sabbath only" congregation. Go beyond the "sacred hours" and you simply will not get a crowd no matter what the special event or how extensive the promotion or programming. Barna's signs of reduced commitments in life include: a climbing divorce rate with half of all new marriages ending in divorce, adults with fewer close friends than adults of earlier decades, reduction in consumer brand loyalty, declining willingness of people to formally "join" any organization, book and record clubs unable to attract new members when multi-year or multi-product commitments are required, dropping percentages of those who consider it their duty to fight for country regardless of the cause, increasing number of "no-shows" to events for which a commitment to attend has been made, parents less likely to believe in the importance of remaining in an unhappy marriage for the sake of the children than 20 years ago.[181]

> ~
>
> Perhaps our greatest challenge is low-level commitment, which is one of the hallmarks of today's society.

It is within this milieu that the church calls people to discipleship, commitment, and sanctification through the empowering of the Holy Spirit. Coming to grips with who we are in relationship to who we ought to be is a sobering and thought-provoking process for our members and especially our church leadership. Assumptions we wished to believe did not hold up when we actually polled ourselves to determine some vital statistics.

The next two chapters are brief summaries of what we have found out about ourselves, our community, our converts, and those whom we will target for future ministry. We have learned things about ourselves that might never have come to the forefront in our thinking if we had not participated in the process.

Chapter 7. Who We Are. A demographic analysis of who makes up our congregation compared with those who make up our community.

Chapter 8. Where We Serve. A demographic understanding of those among whom we live.

Chapter 9. What We Will Do. A demographically-driven proposal aimed at those whom we have best opportunity to reach and to keep.

Who We Are

The Barna Report's annual survey of values and religious views in the United States says that in a typical week, 49 percent of the population say they attend a church worship service, with only 23 percent actually attending some type of religious education class (i.e., Sabbath School or Sunday School) at a church. Also, 27 percent of adults claim that they volunteer some of their personal free time to help a church. In a typical month, 75 percent of all who call themselves Christians attend a church service at least once. Among those who do not attend services at least once monthly, most avoid church altogether: 63 percent say they have not been to church in a year or more, and another 18 percent cannot remember the last time they attended.

Among the self-described Christians who attend church services at least once monthly, 80 percent say they are formal members of the church they most frequently attend. The most common answer given as to why they attend is the desire to worship God (42 percent). Other reasons for church involvement include: to learn more about God (14 percent); to experience personal growth or to become a better person (14 percent); to maintain a tradition of attendance (5 percent); because they enjoy attending (5 percent); response to family pressure (3 percent); to meet new friends (3 percent). About 6 percent of those who attend have no idea why they continue to do so. Not surprisingly, it is the least-rooted population groups that are least likely to become members of a congregation: Baby Busters, singles, GenXers, and those living in Pacific states/provinces in North America.

In an effort to understand ourselves and the unique aspects of our church family in comparison to Christians in general, and other Adventists in particular, the pastoral staff and Marietta church leadership embarked on an intensive self-analysis by surveying our members and regular attendees, our leaders, and especially our new members to determine what factors initially attract newcomers to our congregation and what factors prevent or cause them to leave our congregation. Here are some of our study's results:

What initially attracts newcomers to our congregation?

Responses	*Issue*
56	We are a friendly, outgoing group
51	Broad variety of programming and activities
39	Dynamic, growing environment for young families
38	Quality and vitality of pastoral staff who show care and concern
37	Quality children's programming—Children's Church, Sabbath School, Pathfinders, etc.
35	Quality and spirituality of preaching
34	Reputation of church; recommended by friends
24	Convenient location
23	Doctrines/Beliefs—seeking an Adventist church
22	Facilities
20	Elementary school on campus
12	People seeking crisis help—desperation
6	Music
5	Curiosity
1	Elementary Teachers

What do you think keeps new members involved in our congregation?

63	Quality programming
46	Friendship and fellowship opportunities
40	Involved in church activities and ministries
34	Sermons
34	Pastoral staff
30	Sense of belonging, feel needed
26	Social interaction with others
23	Children's ministries
22	Spiritual tone of congregation and worship services
11	Doctrines—choice to be a Seventh-day Adventist
9	Elementary school (primary school K-8)
8	Outreach emphasis
6	Habit—always been member of Adventist church
4	Music
1	Atlanta Adventist Academy (secondary school 9-12)
1	Facilities

What do you think causes our members to drift away or become inactive

45	Uncared for; indifference exhibited by church members
40	No friends, lack of fellowship, difficult to cross social barriers
35	Uninvolved and not used in ministries

34	Personal problems: guilt, stress, overwork and exhaustion, lack of time, caring for affairs of daily life
24	Personal loss of faith; low personal spirituality
23	Unfriendly atmosphere of congregation, cold, no warmth
20	Criticism of leadership, faultfinding by members of other members, gossip
18	Boredom, uninteresting programs
12	Doctrinal differences
12	Hurt feelings, offended by other members, conflicts with others
11	Apathy, lazy, personal indifference, low motivation
11	Low spirituality of congregation, looking at others instead of Jesus
6	Preference for other Adventist churches
6	Church politics, leadership cliques
4	Not spiritually fed
4	Inadequate programming for young adults
4	Personal health, transportation, distance
3	Irreverence
1	Conflict with pastor
1	Can't see pastor when he preaches at audience level

What could we do to reclaim inactive or former members?

67	Visit and personally encourage their return; invite them to come back
57	Show genuine love, concern, care; make them feel wanted
51	Initiate social interaction; invite them into members' homes
33	Telephone them; let them know they are missed
33	Provide special programs and projects for their participation
18	Pray for their spiritual needs
17	Try to meet their felt needs
16	Exhibit positive attitude toward church. Don't be critical of church leadership; don't share gossip
16	Involve them in small groups and activities; interact with them
16	Accept them as they are; don't be judgmental
14	Provide "help" classes—AA, 12-Step, support groups, prayer fellowships, divorce recovery, singles, etc.
13	Write letters and notes expressing concern and affirmation; send a pamphlet or booklet with notes
9	Provide more youth and young adult programming
8	Listen; be interested in their pain
6	Provide more contemporary worship services
5	Revive spirituality of all members
2	Music
2	Preach doctrinal sermons

1	Preach sermons that speak to the heart
1	Pastor should visit more
1	Advertising
1	Fewer programs; programming not the solution
1	Offer personal counseling

Why do new converts leave the Marietta church?

53	No friends; no network of relationships
43	No support or low support from church members
28	No sense of belonging; social needs not met
26	Feel inferior; cannot measure up to standards, lifestyle changes too great
24	Cannot break into cliques to obtain social interaction
19	Not asked to participate; no appropriate ministries assigned to new members
13	Offended by "superiority" attitude of established members; established members try to correct their lifestyle
13	Inadequate preparation for baptism/membership; low spiritual commitment by new members
13	Inadequate follow-up programs; need new member classes
9	Pull of "old" unspiritual environment and lifestyle
8	Unrealistic expectations by new members for church
6	Established members assume new members are "OK"
4	Apathy; boredom
1	Guest evangelists seem to "abandon" converts when leaving
1	Poor facilities
1	Discouraged because children cannot get into our school

Why do new Adventist transfers leave the Marietta church?

39	No social interaction; cliques have impenetrable barriers
37	Members not inclusive; do not invite new transfers home
27	Feel unneeded
27	We are not a friendly group; new transfers have no friends
16	New transfers get lost in crowd; church too large; impossible to know everyone
15	Unmet expectations
12	Established members are too busy; too preoccupied to expand social circle
11	Socioeconomic/educational differences between transfers and majority of membership
9	Poor facilities; inadequate/overcrowded
8	Apathy of church members toward newcomers
7	New transfers not put into leadership positions or meaningful ministries
6	New transfers are just "church shopping"
6	New transfers are unconverted; over-involved with life-cares

3	New transfers are shy
3	Don't like school
3	No formal assimilation process
2	Don't like pastor/worship service style
1	Offended by established members

What can we do to keep and nurture new converts in our church?

42	Elders provide more intentional spiritual guardianship
34	Leaders invite new members into their homes; fellowship with them and get to know them
33	Get new converts involved in group activities and social functions with other members
27	Get new converts involved in ministry activities
23	Make them feel wanted; sit with them; telephone them
20	Provide new member class; new member groups
17	Make them feel needed in life of congregation
14	Leaders should personally encourage them—attendance; provide shelter from criticism; barrier to fanatical members who lead them astray
11	Seek feedback about their needs; listen to them
11	More public introductions to church family; name tags, flowers, greeters, etc.
7	Provide better instruction/preparation for baptism
3	Pray for them
3	Provide new member orientation packets
3	Teach established members "obedience" of caring for new members; it is God's will that they care for newcomers
1	Hire a pastor for visitation
1	Need better facilities

Our discovery

The first thing we discovered about ourselves is that we knew much more about what we ought to be doing with regard to assimilating new members than we were actually doing. Like so many other areas of theology, we needed to put legs on our beliefs and set them into action in the arena of daily life rather than keeping accurate understandings confined to the theoretical or hypothetical.

The most significant result was the clear indication that we already had sufficient knowledge concerning our problems to intentionally drive the design and implementation of appropriate solutions. In other words, the responses to the questions identified the issues, affirmed what we had already documented from the literature, and gave guidance for what we needed to do to better assimilate our members.

Our intentions were clear. Would our actions be consistent with these intentions? Perhaps the more sobering question was whether or not we

~

We knew more
about what
we ought to do
than we were
actually doing.

~

were willing to pay the price to accomplish the changes that were necessary if we wished to achieve the results we wanted.

One of the processes by which we arrived at this determination to better assimilate our new members occurred at the earliest stages of negotiation between congregation and pastor–when we "considered each other"and Sharon and I accepted the invitation of the conference to serve as pastors.

Although it was clear that the conference organization appointed pastors, we had the unique privilege of an extensive interaction process through which the congregation shared its dreams and hopes for the future and, as prospective pastors, we had the privileged opportunity to determine if our vision and their dreams would mesh.

Such interaction between potential pastors and congregations is becoming increasingly prevalent among Seventh-day Adventists, particularly in large, professionally-oriented congregations. Wise conference leaders have learned that they accomplish little if they merely exercise their power to appoint pastors without such consultation. I applaud the openness with which many conference administrators allow such a process to occur. Our decision to accept this pastoral assignment was predicated on the congregation's response to a church growth study of both attitudes and abilities resident in the congregation with regard to the potential for change.

Toward a change

Increasingly, the emphasis on the pastor as an agent for change will determine the success or failure of "buy in" by the congregation. Larry L. McSwain discusses the need for a theology of change as an undergirding basis for pastoral formation. He sees three processes of change that focus on three specific issues:

Centering: The identity of the minister as an agent of change requires the kind of commitment which seeks changes consistent with God's will as revealed in Scripture. In this focus, the pastor does not merely react to the changing values of society, but rather, as an intentional person, identifies who or what needs to be changed and, then, centers on those life-and-death concerns which affect the persons and institutions served. The question to be asked here is, "Who are you as a minister of the gospel engaged in change?"

Prophetic Critique: The second process of a ministry of change focuses on a rejection of the status quo. If the minister's life is centered upon seeking God's will for the individual members and the community of believers together, then there must be a rejection of life as it is found. The need for change, whether at the individual or social level, is a judgment upon the status quo. The pastor's responsibility as a change agent is to identify the will of God *vis-a-vis* the present behavior of individuals and groups. Ministers must guard carefully that their own opinions do not become equated with prophetic edicts, which is why "centering" is the vital first step. Thus, the second question, "What needs changing?," must come only after the pastor knows who he/she is in relationship to God's call.

Construction: The third process for effecting changes requires practical strategies for moving from the need for change to a Christian response. One does not criticize for the sake of intellectual cynicism. The purpose of prophetic critique is to awaken the will of those needing to change to develop constructive plans to do something different. This third focus requires the church to seek God's way in place of our own way. It also means living within the community of believers as if God's future promises have already been received. The question here is much more than "What shall we do someday?" The question is, "How shall we now live so that we may someday become what God's intention has in store for us." [182]

> How shall
> we live now so
> that we may someday
> become what
> God intends?

After careful initial analysis, I believed the Marietta congregation desired pastoral leadership for change and were willing to pay the price to accomplish the changes they wanted. Based on this evaluation and subsequent actions of the church's leadership, I accepted the invitation to serve as pastor at Marietta with a broad-based mandate to effect change.

The perspective of passing years, which have included a dramatic change in my own assignment from local pastor to an executive post at our denomination's world headquarters, have proven the point. The Marietta congregation has continued to flourish and continues to utilize the plans we developed in a variety of areas, including new member assimilation. In fact, under the leadership of its current pastoral team, this church has accomplished far more than I could have dreamed, and I was "dreaming big!"

For me, the two most rewarding comments on my ministry at Marietta came from the chair of our board of elders upon my departure and from the pastor who succeeded me about one year after his arrival. The head elder stated, "Your leadership in our midst set a new standard. Every time we thought we had achieved what you envisioned, you raised the mark a bit higher and motivated us to become much more than we believed we could be. Your vision became our commitment." My successor stated that he had never pastored a church more prepared, at the beginning of his tenure, to move forward. He reckoned that Marietta had a two-year advance over his previous congregations in their readiness to embrace progress.

> ∼
> **Assimilating new members is one component of an overall church growth strategy.**
> ∼

How did this all come about? Early on, significant steps were taken by the church's operating board, even before the specifics of this plan were developed. In fact, it is vital to understand this assimilation plan as one component part of an overall strategy for church growth. These significant actions by church leadership were not limited to new member assimilation, but rather they supported the whole vision of change for our congregation. They included:

1. Conducting a visioning weekend for church leaders. The results of this weekend brought a determination to grow the congregation numerically and spiritually, to restore the financial base of the congregation to a position of strength, and to better nurture our new members.

2. Establishing a theme, *Building a Life in Focus,* that emphasized growth, spiritual development, and priorities. Although borrowed from a slogan developed by the president of the Southern Union, we expressed this in terms and actions particularly unique to our setting.

3. Developing short-term strategies to meet immediate needs, while searching for long-term solutions. For example, immediate financial crisis was managed without short-changing the essential resources needed to fuel our plans for growth.

4. Approving an extensive process to develop long-term strategies which have produced this plan as one, among several areas, needing strong improvement.

5. Selecting individuals from, and electing new members to, the board of elders who were gifted and committed to forming a New Member Assimilation Committee. This subcommittee was charged with the specific task of developing action plans to care for new members.

6. Appointing a Pastor-Parish Relationship Committee to provide specific and encouraging nurture for pastoral leadership throughout the change process.

7. Appointing a Committee of Concern, a subcommittee of the board of elders, with the assignment to hear complaints, to shield the pastoral staff from unjust criticism from those resisting change, to hear and adjudicate conflicts between members, or to bring recommendations to the elders if disciplinary action was needed.

> Vision what the church "can be" more than lamenting the problems of "where we are."

8. Agreement that laity leaders would consistently talk in visioning terms of "what we can be" rather than focusing on the problems of "where we are." Church leaders were determined to be viewed as future bound!

These and myriad other indications of corporate willingness to change, along with wide congregational support for pastoral leadership's implementation of a change process, made this entire process much more enjoyable and personally motivating than might be imagined.

While it is necessary to identify the widespread attitudes of lethargy, satisfaction with the status quo, and preoccupation with competing agendas that were as prevalent in our congregation as any other, it is equally important to stress the overall willingness of the members to be led by their leaders into spiritual ventures different from their previous experiences. It was this readiness to deal seriously with spiritual issues and to move forward, despite the costs, which guaranteed the success of this plan.

Chapter 8

Where We Are

How did the demographic statistics of the Marietta church compare with those of the surrounding community?

In recent decades Cobb County has become a bedroom community for the greater Atlanta metropolitan area rather than an employment center in its own right. While Cobb is Georgia's number one county in resident income, it is only fourth in terms of wages paid to those who earn their living in county.[183] The general population, like the majority of our congregants, travel to Atlanta to earn their living. Obviously, this one-hour-plus daily commute should determine different strategies for evangelism and nurture from those that might be used if the major share of our members or the county's population lived and worked close to home.

The following chart displays current population statistics for Cobb County by age groupings compared with our congregants by age grouping:

Age	Population	Percentage	Our members
0 - 19	129,211	27.2%	33.2%
20 - 39	213,809	44.9%	38.7%
40 - 59	95,333	20.1%	21.6%
60+	37,234	7.8%	6.5%
Totals	475,587	100.0%[184]	100.0%[185]

These figures demonstrate why our congregation, appropriately, invested much of its staff, money, and programming—both evangelistic and nurture activities—on issues and projects designed to meet the needs of young families. Such programs included parochial elementary and secondary education, children's church, youth worship services, summer daycamp programs, Pathfinder and Adventure clubs, Vacation Bible School, softball, volleyball, other sports activities, summer internships for college-age students, work-study program for high school students, as well as special weekends for youth, etc.

Of course, one of the challenges for the next twenty years will be to adapt the services and programs which the church provides to the inevitable graying of our membership and the population, while still remaining relevant to our young families. After all, today's nineteen year old will still be under the age of forty in twenty years.

Racial characteristics of Cobb County show 411,689 (93.2 percent) Caucasian and 29,974 (6.8 percent) African-American or other.[186] This was also reflected in Marietta whose congregation was 94 percent Caucasian and 6 percent African-American or other. However, our Caucasian membership's racial makeup says less about our commitment to racial interaction than is reality. A few years earlier, we would have had a larger percentage of non-Caucasian members, but since 1989 new Black, Korean, and Spanish congregations have begun in Cobb County, with many of the members of these new churches coming from our congregation. Perhaps this change does more to validate the church growth principle of homogeneity than it says about any exclusiveness. Nevertheless, membership acceptance

> Understanding ourselves is just the first step in intentionally targeting those whom we can reach.

of individuals from other races was an easier task to accomplish than full integration in the life of the congregation. This reality may have spurred the formation of these new ethnic congregations.

Cobb County's educational levels are among the highest in the Atlanta metropolitan area, with high school graduates comprising 72.3 percent of the population and college graduates (or beyond) making up 22.9 percent. Furthermore, in the areas where most of our members reside, these percentages increased to 91.8 percent high school graduates and 42.1 percent college (or beyond) graduates.[187] With the strong emphasis that Adventists place on education, particularly parochial education from pre-school through university, it should not surprise us to discover that our own congregation exceeded the highest levels in the county for educational attainments. Over 90 percent of adult Marietta members are high school graduates and nearly two-thirds (65 percent) are college graduates.

Targeting outreach

Understanding ourselves in relationship to our community, however, is just the first step in intentionally targeting those whom we can reach. Rick Warren, senior pastor of Orange County's Saddleback Valley Community Church stresses the necessity of targeting potential members. "There is not a local church anywhere that can reach everybody . . . To reach all of these people for Christ will require a variety of styles of evangelism." [188] Warren refuses to debate which methods of evangelism work best because it depends upon who the church is trying to reach. He says, "The Bible determines our message, but our target determines when, where, and how we communicate it." [189] The strategy for Saddleback Valley was to figure out who the church was best capable of reaching for Jesus Christ and then to intentionally go after those people.

Furthermore, Warren points out that targeting for evangelism is biblical by offering the examples of:

Jesus: "I was sent only to the lost sheep of Israel" (Matt. 15:24).

Disciples: "Do not go among the Gentiles or enter any town of the Samaritans. Go rather to the lost sheep of Israel" (Matt. 10:5-6).

Paul and Peter: "I had been entrusted with the task of preaching the gospel to the Gentiles, just as Peter had been to the Jews" (Gal. 2:7).

Gospel Commission: We are to make disciples of "all nations." The term *ta ethne,* from which we derive the word *ethnic,* refers literally to "all people groups." Each of these unique people groups needs an evangelistic strategy that communicates the gospel in terms that their specific culture can understand. [190]

As Warren points out, one of the advantages of large churches is that they possess resources sufficient to go after multiple targets. The larger the church, the more choices can be offered. Nevertheless, determining to target and defining the target audience is essential for growth. He gives four specific ways to define the target for a congregation: geographically, demographically, culturally, and spiritually [191] and describes the composite profile of the typically unchurched individual his congregation has targeted.

Using the descriptive "Saddleback Sam, married to Saddleback Samantha with two children," Warren lists the components of those individuals his church is most able to reach:

- well educated
- likes his job
- likes where he lives
- high priority for health and fitness
- prefers large groups to small groups
- skeptical of "organized" religion
- likes contemporary music
- thinks he enjoys life more today than he did five years ago
- self-satisfied, even smug, about his station in life
- prefers the casual and informal over the formal
- overextended in both time and money [192]

Warren concludes that the more focused the church's target, the more likely it will be able to hit it. He challenges the church to find its own composite *Dallas Doug, London Larry, Melbourne Mac,* or *Rio Ronaldo.* Otherwise, the church is like a photographer who takes pictures without first focusing or a deer hunter shooting randomly without taking aim. "Without a target, our efforts at evangelism are often only wishful thinking." [193]

The emphasis and helpful instruction provided by Rick Warren prompts us to recognize the validity of the homogenous principle—like will best win like. The advantage for our Marietta church was that the composite *Marietta Mitch* already closely resembled the makeup of our membership.

Warren mentions another issue that must be comprehended and dealt with—society's increasing ambivalence to denominational identity. For Seventh-day Adventists, this has been a particularly bitter pill to swallow since we have a long-established subculture which has self-identified and self-authenticated our reason for existence. As we have described in Chapter 4, this historical stance of Seventh-day Adventists is crumbling in the reality of today's society. Marietta church was far down that road due to a number of

> ∿
> ## Can Adventist churches experience significant growth and still maintain their traditionally strong denominational identity?
> ∿

factors, including a highly mobile membership, affluent families, third- and fourth-generation Seventh-day Adventists, as well as the various other factors that affect every denomination.

Growth and church identity

Can Seventh-day Adventist churches experience significant growth and still maintain their traditionally strong denominational identity? Lyle Schaller describes three types of religious traditions based on polity:

a. Authority centralized at the headquarters of the denomination with an elaborate system of polity rules and regulations (i.e., Roman Catholic Church or Presbyterian Church U.S.A.).

b. Authority partly connectional and partly congregational in polity (i.e., Reformed Church in America, Episcopal Church, Evangelical Lutheran Church).

c. Authority resides completely in the local congregation with autonomous decision making always occurring at the congregational level (i.e. the plethora of independent churches, or very loose alliances, which have sprung up in recent years). [194]

Documenting the increased population of the United States coupled with the reduction in the number of congregations by several mainstream religious traditions, Schaller asserts that an urgent need has been created for planting new churches. Who has filled this vacuum? Primarily the independent, congregational-polity-based churches. However, Schaller says one of the strongest efforts by any one religious tradition came from the Southern Baptists, who reported a net gain of 4,500 congregations during the twenty-five years between 1968 and 1993. As another example, he adds, Seventh-day Adventists, "a connectional-polity denomination, experienced a net increase of more than a thousand congregations." [195]

> An
> urgent need
> has been created
> for planting
> new churches.

While Schaller clearly sees the cutting edge of growth with the totally independent, or congregational-polity churches, these two examples demonstrate that it is possible to achieve significant growth within the framework of the partly connectional-polity tradition. Although Adventists may be much closer to the centralized polity tradition at the conference level, we can affirm our ability to achieve significant growth without abandoning the distinctive self-understanding and self-identity we possess.

Therefore, since our membership at Marietta was an apt reflection of the community in which we resided in terms of age, economic strength, racial balance, religious experience, and educational attainments, there was no logical reason why we should not grow at a faster rate than our present attainment nor why we should not easily attract new members from our neighbors in our community. The task is to develop strategies in harmony both with who we are as well as with those whom we expect to reach.

Chapter 9

What We Will Do

What shall we do? Perhaps the greatest challenge of introspection is not to realize who we are but to grapple with what we will do, if anything, concerning what we have discovered about ourselves.

Even a cursory glance at Marietta's demographics showed a congregation that was very comfortable, with little reason to upset the status quo by an aggressive program to reach the lost or even to assimilate those who, somehow, came to the church. Except for the convictions of a small percentage of the membership—thankfully, most of these were leaders—Marietta church could have remained on the plateau of status quo maintenance for the foreseeable future. No need was seen for growth. In fact, many members viewed growth as more of a bother than a benefit.

Evangelism seemed to be tolerated because the gospel commission appeared to be important to the pastoral staff, who were generally appreciated and affirmed by the members as "steering us in the right direction." Ideas and programs that would be openly rejected from an unpopular or weak pastor were endured because of the real affection expressed toward pastoral leadership. For the first two years of my pastorate, church growth was viewed as primarily "the pastor's agenda" and tolerance was stated in terms such as "all this outreach stuff seems really important to Pastor Jim and, after all, he never does anything to embarrass us." In short, it seemed a small thing for members to tolerate my passion in exchange for better pastoral care than their recent lengthy interim had provided.

Ours was a large congregation compared with the typical Adventist congregation in North America. Our members generally were young, affluent, and over extended in time, finances, and emotional baggage. They were politically conservative, liberal in lifestyle issues, and had a "live and let live" attitude toward fellow church members as well as the community around us. A prevalent attitude toward new members might well have been expressed as, "If they stick it out, good for them! If they don't, too bad. We didn't really need them anyway!"

In retrospect, a sizeable number of our congregants might have analyzed their spiritual journey in sufficient depth to describe themselves as Adventists more by heritage than by conviction—a typical Adventist shibboleth is "Laodicean."

Such members would not lack certain convictions. They would readily embrace the concept that Adventists are theologically correct even as they would neglect spiritual disciplines in which the Living Word impacts their daily lives. A clear compartmentalization of life into business and related social activities over against church and related social activities would be the norm for too many members. The idea of all-pervasive discipleship would be foreign to the reality of their daily existence.

While they would reject the term "nominal," these members have seldom confronted the issues of personal discipleship, much less the commission to reach others. Having been raised and educated within the Adventist system, it is easier to remain within the subculture of Adventism for religious experience and social interaction than to face disappointment and recrimination from parents or friends should they exit membership. Many of our members began to wrestle with personal discipleship only during our intentional process of confronting who we were.

However, this had not been without significant progress. By focusing preaching toward personal spiritual growth and emphasizing the components of Bible study, prayer, fellowship, witnessing, and obedience, 71 percent of our members indicated that their personal responsiveness to God's expectations for their lives was greater than one year earlier.

Various trends indicated this was a valid observation. Attendance had increased in both services. Tithe (denomination funds) and offerings (local congregational funds) rose significantly. Community involvement had never been more active, and our members participated in a variety of felt-need or service-oriented ministries.

As our board of elders analyzed what we might do to intentionally assimilate more new members and stabilize those we already had who were spiritually weak, we devised the following proposal to support our strategy of conserving our catch.

Conserving the catch
Our proposal was designed around three demographic-based concepts:
1. *We built on our demographic strengths:*
a. A congregation younger than the typical Seventh-day Adventist church would have increased expectations that programming would be family-focused with special nurture provided for children ages 0-14. For example, weekly worship services for children, special worship services

for youth, as well as child-care provisions at all events became the norm.

b. A congregation more affluent than the typical Seventh-day Adventist church would have increased expectations that facilities and programming would be measured by quality as much as by quantity. For example, members financially sponsoring and hosting various events provided by technical specialists became the norm. A long-overdue renovation and upgrading of the entire physical plant was also begun and progressive expansion has continued.

c. A congregation more educated than the typical Seventh-day Adventist church would have increased expectations that programming would address the real-life situation in which members and their neighbors existed rather than consist of generic plans provided by the denomination's bureaucracy. For example, instead of door-to-door literature distribution or revival meetings, we offered evangelistic activities in seminar, lecture, or study-group format. It is essential to remember that form is less important than functions which have become the norm through historical validation.

d. A congregation more overextended in time commitments than the typical Seventh-day Adventist church would have increased expectations that tasks which typically might be provided by volunteers would, instead, be accomplished by employees. For example, the board voted additional budgetary provisions to hire visitation pastors, children's ministries leaders, secretaries, musicians, cooks, technicians, and child-care providers.

2. *We ministered to and with the community in which we resided:*

a. A membership younger than the typical Seventh-day Adventist church would sponsor programming such as summer day camp, Mom's Day Out, parenting seminars, and family-inclusive events more than sewing circles, bus tours, or prayer meetings.

b. A congregation more affluent than the typical Seventh-day Adventist church would contribute to relief centers coordinated by all the churches of the community rather than operating an on-campus facility, despite the longstanding Adventist tradition of crisis-care Dorcas societies. For example, we would likely sponsor inner-city children to summer camp, provide after-school work activities for students needing to earn tuition, or fund the community food bank more than we would open the doors of our sanctuary for use as a homeless shelter which would only replicate the services of the community shelter less than one-half mile away.

c. A congregation more educated than the typical Seventh-day Adventist church would provide quality refreshments for members and guests before services or secure the services of featured experts or artists more than home-spun productions such as a "we did it ourselves" Easter pageant. We would rely on consistent advertising in the news media and through signs and direct mailing brochures more than on overt solicitation of individuals to attend events.

   d. A congregation more overextended in time commitments than the typical Seventh-day Adventist church would have increased expectations that organizational coordination, tight time controls, proscribed program lengths, etc., would take precedence over a "we'll finish when we get there" attitude. For example, we discovered that our leaders and members were more readily available to attend several events stacked upon one another in the same Sabbath than they were to return for the same events scheduled throughout the week.

3.   *We ministered beyond the limitations that our own history and proclivities might dictate.* We developed activities that stretched us beyond our comfort zone. Only thus could we truly reach and hold our new members.

   a. A congregation younger than the typical Seventh-day Adventist church would have members form an energy core that, if tapped, could unleash great potential for appropriate nurture activities such as home-based fellowship and study groups or an Assimilation Taskforce.

   b. A congregation more affluent than the typical Seventh-day Adventist church would have members with sufficient financial resources to obtain for themselves creative curriculum materials and personal study/ growth opportunities. For example, they could afford to invite a coworker or neighbor to attend a special program or sharing event.

   c. A congregation more educated than the typical Seventh-day Adventist church would have members whose personal capabilities, if tapped, enable them to become effective spokespersons for the power of God rather than relying on the pastoral staff or itinerating evangelists to proclaim the gospel.

   d. A congregation more overextended in time commitments than the typical Seventh-day Adventist church would have members with innate organizational skills to accomplish much in a short time. By prioritizing fellowship and witnessing as part of their self-expected performance, they would schedule and accomplish more than someone else, whose life is less structured, might even attempt.

   In conclusion, as we developed this strategy proposal and the activities outlined in the following chapters, we were convicted that the Holy Spirit had already gifted our congregation with whatever resources we needed to accomplish our Heavenly Father's will for our church. Whether we utilized these gifts to accomplish His objectives was to be seen. The provisions, however, were sufficient. As Ellen White says, "As the will of man cooperates with the will of God, it becomes omnipotent. Whatever is to be done at His command may be accomplished in His strength. All His biddings are enablings!" [196]

~ **Part IV** ~

Practical, Doable Plans

I love the word "doable," which I first heard Pastor Charles E. Bradford use to describe practical action as more than mere conceptualization. "Doable" means moving beyond the theoretical to implementation. This is a challenge for any organization. As Pastor Bradford also stated, "The church is especially challenged to live between the *is* and the *ought.*"

It is not too challenging to recognize what we "ought to be" or even to describe what "is." Seldom is there a total lack of recognition for what a church ought to be doing even if the church is not presently functioning at that capacity. But doing something about the situation is another matter entirely.

For our church family at Marietta, the desire to do God's will in relationship to caring for newly-accessioned members became a reality as we moved from concept to strategy to implementation.

The following three chapters are indicative of what we tried to accomplish, and even succeeded in implementing, as our activities were intentionally focused toward assimilating new members into the life of our congregation rather than merely adding them to our membership rolls.

Chapter 10. Methods for integrating new transfers. Our intent was to activate those Adventists who transfer to Marietta into participatory fellowship in our church family.

Chapter 11. Methods for integrating new believers . Our intent was to build those new believers who became members at Marietta into disciples who serve Christ in the context of our church family.

Chapter 12. Methods for bidding farewell to departing members. Our intent was to to affirm and recognize the ministry of those who move to another congregation so that they can be active in participatory fellowship in the new church.

The methods that we employed and the lessons we learned can well serve any church.

Chapter 10

Methods for Integrating New Transfers

Our experience at Marietta church showed us several creative and meaningful ways that motivated Seventh-day Adventists who visited our church to choose to join our fellowship and to become participatory in the fellowship of our church family. We summarize these methods under three areas (invitation, initiation, and integration) and are confident that they can work in any church.

Invitation

1. Utilize the "green card" (our in-congregation reference name to a registration/response form which we used weekly) at all worship services. This card includes an invitation for Adventists, especially those new to the community, to transfer membership to your congregation.

2. Contact all registered Adventist guests with a letter of greeting, a pastoral telephone call, and a visit by a church elder.

3. Add all registered guests to your mailing list data base to receive your weekly church newsletter.

Initiation

1. Acknowledge all requests for transfer with personal contact by pastoral staff.

2. Assign incoming transfer members to a church elder's care group.

3. Present each transfer request to the church board for action, to the membership clerk for processing a transfer-of-membership letter from the previous church, and for subsequent publication of the transfer in the church bulletin. By common consent, the third weekly publication of any transfer becomes an official vote of the congregation.

4. Greet each new transferee with a welcome letter from the pastor and a membership survey which solicits background information,

opinions, and suggestions as well as areas in which the transferee anticipates ministering.

5. Introduce each new transferee to the congregation during a Sabbath worship service. Pastoral staff will interview each new transferee and welcome them with an appropriate gift book.

6. Invite each new transferee to stand with the pastoral staff at the primary exit to receive the greetings and introductions of members.

7. Change the code on the church database from guest to member. Add the new transferee to the conference records and subscription list for the union paper.

> Add all registered guests to your mailing list database.

Integration

1. Assign the elder in whose care group the new member is registered to sponsor or see to implementation of three social interaction events within the first two months of membership.

2. Schedule the newly-transferred member to participate in a New Member Orientation which consists of the following components:

a. Luncheon provided at least quarterly, more often if needed, by assimilation committee for all new members plus church board.

b. Welcome and introductions by senior pastor plus a descriptive and prescriptive process for continuing spiritual growth.

c. Historical presentation about our church, concluding with our vision for the future.

d. Description of ministry opportunities and current special projects and/or needs of the congregation.

e. Relaxed social interaction at conclusion.

3. Commemorate the first anniversary of transferee with a special greeting from the pastor.

4. Solicit input at any time from the elder-in-charge if more specific spiritual nurture is needed.

Chapter 11

Methods for Integrating New Believers

Once again we turn to our experience in Marietta church–how experience taught us and helped us in integrating new believers into the life, worship, and fellowship of the church. The methods that helped us in integrating new believers are summarized, as in the previous chapter dealing with transferees, under the categories of invitation, initiation, and integration. We believe these methods will help integrate newly baptized members into participatory fellowship in any church family, as they did in our own.

Invitation

1. Utilize the "green card" registration form at all worship services. This card includes an invitation to accept Jesus Christ as Saviour, offers a pastoral visit, and provides opportunity to request baptism and church membership.

2. Contact all registered guests with a letter of greeting and a pastoral telephone call.

3. Add all registered guests to your mailing list database to receive your weekly church newsletter.

Initiation

1. Honor each request for acceptance of Christ, pastoral visit, baptism, or church membership with quick response from pastoral staff.

2. Assign potential members to a church elder's care group and invite the elder to visit the potential member with the pastor.

3. Request assigned elder to prepare each potential member for baptism or membership in accordance with their wishes and their spiritual development, using resources such as:

a. Bible workbook series for children.

b. Bible guides, *27 Fundamental Beliefs, In His Steps* for adults.

4. Schedule a personal interview with the pastoral staff when the potential member has completed the preparation process.

5. Plan the baptism celebration for an appropriate date.

6. Provide each baptismal candidate with embossed invitations with which they can invite their family and friends to be present for their baptism.

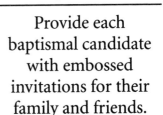

> Provide each baptismal candidate with embossed invitations for their family and friends.

7. Conduct each baptism in a spiritually significant way which includes appropriate components from the following options:

a. Introduce the candidate to the church family.

b. Relate the story of this individual's experience with Jesus.

c. Affirm the process of the new member's decision and preparation for baptism.

d. Welcome the new member by a congregational vote of affirmation.

e. Recognize any family or friends present at this service.

f. Invite others who are present to consider this step for their own lives.

8. Greet each new member with a welcome letter from the pastor and a membership survey which solicits background information, opinions, and suggestions as well as areas in which the new member anticipates ministering.

9. Introduce each new member to the congregation during a Sabbath worship service. Pastoral staff will interview each new member, present their baptismal certificate, and welcome them with an appropriate gift book.

10. Invite each new member to stand with the pastoral staff at the primary exit to receive the greetings and introductions of members.

11. Change the code from guest to member on the church database. Add the new member to the conference records and subscription list for the union paper.

12. Order gift subscriptions for each new member to the *Adventist Review* and *Signs of the Times.*

Integration

1. Assign the elder in whose care group the new member is registered to sponsor or see to implementation of three social interaction events within the first two months of membership.

2. Schedule the newly transferred member to participate in a New Member Orientation which consists of the following components:

a. Luncheon provided at least quarterly, more often if needed, by assimilation committee for all new members plus church board.

b. Welcome and introductions by senior pastor plus a process prescription for continuing spiritual growth.

c. Historical presentation of our church, concluding with our vision for the future.

d. Description of ministry opportunities and current special projects and/or needs of the congregation.

e. Relaxed social interaction at conclusion.

Enroll
each new believer
in
discipleship
classes.

3. Provide a weekly letter from the pastor to each new member. See Appendix for sample letters.

4. Assign a trained member of the Assimilation Taskforce to serve as a special friend for the new believer. Specific assignments are to be completed on a weekly basis by each special friend on behalf of the new believer assigned to their care (see Appendix A).

5. Enroll the new believer in a new members class, to be followed by a spiritual gifts discovery class, to be followed by a training-for-service workshop.

6. Commemorate the first anniversary of baptism with a special greeting from the pastor.

7. Solicit input from the elder-in-charge or special friend at any time more specific spiritual nurture is needed.

Chapter 12

Methods for Bidding Farewell to Departing Members

In today's highly mobile society, members easily move from one church to another. Marietta was no exception. Recognizing that an important part of spiritual nurture includes helping members re-establish and maintain fellowship when they relocate, we believe certain methods helped our church family appropriately care for those leaving our area. Our objective was to encourage their quick integration into participatory fellowship in another church family. We summarize those methods under the categories of process and follow-through and believe that these will help your church as well.

Process
1. Announce the planned departure to the congregation through the newsletter or other appropriate communication.
2. Recognize the contribution that the departing member has made to your congregation by a certificate of appreciation to be presented during worship services.
3. Invite departing members to stand with the pastoral staff at the primary exit to receive best wishes from the members.
4. Recommend that the elder's care group which has provided nurture for this family appropriately farewell their departure.

Follow-through
1. Send a letter from the pastoral staff to the pastor of the church nearest the new location of departing members. Include a summary of the talents and service contributions of the departing members.

2. Suggest a transfer of membership to departing members if they do not self-initiate this process. Explain that our objective is for them to become established in participatory fellowship in a new congregation.

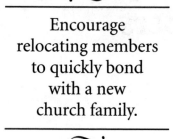

Encourage relocating members to quickly bond with a new church family.

3. Process transfer requests for departing members with quick response to encourage their participation in their new congregation.

4. Write transferred members after their relocation to encourage their faithfulness and fellowship in their new church family.

5.   Keep transferred members on the weekly newsletter mailing list for a minimum of six months after their transfer is completed.

6. Keep transferred members perpetually on an annual mailing list to share a yearly summary of news of their "home" church.

7. Invite former members to return on appropriate occasions such as anniversaries, etc.

Conclusion

When Jesus called His church to disciple the nations, He asked far more to be accomplished than just the proclamation of good news. He asked the church to model the kingdom in the world as a witness and as a preferable alternative to the world's agenda.

Today, as then, the church must state to secular society that the body of Christ is preferable to the chaos of Satan. This message will not be effectively communicated or really believed unless our treatment of new members demonstrates God's care for them to be vastly superior to what they would find elsewhere.

> Every church must do something different and better than we have done previously.

For Christians, nurture is not everything. But for new Christians, nurture is the only thing that will allow them to mature to the point that they can participate in ministry themselves.

This book's conclusion, therefore, is essentially a beginning. Growing from the proposals described here, implementation of our strategies must become more than mere intellectual exercise or mental gymnastics.

From this day forward our church, indeed every church in our whole denomination, must do something different and better than we have done previously. If we do not perform in different and better ways than we have previously treated new members, this book is a failure; more so, our church will be a failure.

Knowing what to do, without doing what we should, falls short of the objectives at the peril of people lost to the kingdom.

It is my prayer that this study and the implementation of its principles will hasten the return of Jesus by better caring for those who are first seeking to know Him, whom to know is life eternal!

Endnotes

[1] James F. Engel and Wilbert Norton, *What's Gone Wrong With the Harvest?*, 45 (See Appendix A).

[2] C. Peter Wagner, *Strategies for Church Growth*, 128.

[3] Gary Land, ed., *Adventism in America*, 209.

[4] C. Peter Wagner. My personal class notes from lecture in Church Growth I, March, 1986.

[5] Allen Hadidian, *Discipleship: Helping Other Christians Grow*, 11.

[6] Myron S. Augsburger, *Matthew*, 330.

[7] Donald A. McGavran, *Understanding Church Growth*, 74.

[8] *Ibid.*, 169-170.

[9] Hadidian, 29.

[10] *Ibid.*, Modification to include "friendship" mine. Hadidian omits friendship in his diagram as being self-evident in the process. I believe the addition helps!

[11] *Ibid.*, 12-20.

[12] In C. Peter Wagner, Win Arn, and Elmer Towns, *Church Growth: The State of the Art*, 58-59.

[13] C. Peter Wagner, *Your Church Can Be Healthy*, 69.

[14] Sherwood Eliot Wirt, ed., *Evangelism: The Next Ten Years*, 103-104.

[15] Walter A. Henrichsen, *Disciples are Made—Not Born*, 52.

[16] J. D. Douglas, ed., *The Work of an Evangelist*, 193.

[17] In Wagner, *Church Growth: State of the Art*, 57-58.

[18] C. Peter Wagner, *Your Church Can Grow*, 161.

[19] W. Oscar Thompson, Jr., *Concentric Circles of Concern*, 156.

[20] Billy Graham, *A Biblical Standard for Evangelists*, 109.

[21] An expanded discussion of needed instruction is provided in Chapter 4.

[22] Engel and Norton, 54.

[23] Carl Wilson, *With Christ in the School of Disciple Making*, 211.

[24] Eddie Gibbs, *I Believe in Church Growth*, 321.

[25] *Ibid.*, 322.

[26] Richard John Neuhaus, *Freedom for Ministry*, 99.

[27] George W. Peters, *A Theology of Church Growth*, 201.

[28] George E. Sweazey, *The Church as Evangelist*, 193.

[29] *Ibid.*

[30] *Ibid.*, 194.

[31] Ben Campbell Johnson, *Rethinking Evangelism*, 95.

[32] George Barna, *User Friendly Churches*, 72.

[33] *Ibid.*

[34] Roger L. Dudley and Des Cummings, Jr., *Adventures in Church Growth*, 33-34.

[35] William Martin, *A Prophet With Honor*, 550.

[36] Wilson, 219.

[37] Graham, 110-111.

[38] Keith M. Bailey, *Care of Converts*, 14-15.

[39] Henrichsen, 79-80.

[40] John R. W. Stott, *The Christian Mission in the Modern World*, 114.

[41] *Ibid.*, 114-115. Emphasis mine.

[42] *Ibid.*, 115-116.

[43] Sweazey, 193.

[44] Engel and Norton, 54-55.

[45] Henrichsen, 79.

[46] Carl M. Sweazy, *Evangelism that Evangelizes*, 57.

[47] In *Ibid.*

[48] Johnson, 95.

[49] Engel and Norton, 52.

[50] Charles L. Chaney and Ron S. Lewis, *Design for Church Growth*.

[51] C. Peter Wagner, *Church Growth and the Whole Gospel*, 140.

[52] Ogilvie, 179.

[53] Dudley and Cummings, 135.

[54] *Ibid.*

[55] Myron Widmer, "My Friends, the Missing," *Adventist Review* (May 4, 1989), 5.

[56] Sweazy, 63-64.

57 William G. Johnsson, "The Missing Tell Us Why," *Adventist Review* (September 7, 1989), 8.

58 Widmer.

59 Dudley and Cummings, 136.

60 Jerry Cook with Stanley C. Baldwin, *Love, Acceptance and Forgiveness*, 35-54.

61 Bruce Johnston, "A Myth Is as Good as a Mile: All New Converts Soon Leave," *North Pacific Union Gleaner* (November 6, 1989), 4.

62 *Ibid.*

63 Linford Lee Martin, *The Challenge of the Empty Pew*, 77-78.

64 *Ibid.*, 78.

65 Dudley and Cummings, 146-148.

66 Almost all new members in earlier years came from other churches because the population in general was more strongly churched than today. Typically new Adventists today come from an unchurched background.

67 Ellen G. White, *Evangelism*, 351.

68 John W. Fowler, "Caring for New Converts," *Ministry* (April, 1979), 4.

69 *Ibid.*

70 Dudley and Cummings, 148-149.

71 Widmer.

72 George Barna, *The Frog in the Kettle*, 223.

73 Mike Bellah, *Baby Boom Believers*, 132.

74 Frank R. Tillapaugh, *Unleashing the Church*, 60-61.

75 *Ibid.*, 130.

76 Sharon M. Cress, "Why Members Leave," *PRAXIS* (Summer, 1987), 13.

77 John R. Stott, *Christian Mission in the Modern World*, 119.

78 Donald A. McGavran and Winfield C. Arn, *Ten Steps for Church Growth*, 81.

79 Carl George, *Empty Pews, Empty Streets*, 50-51.

80 *Ibid.*, 51.

81 McGavran and Arn, *Ten Steps for Church Growth*, 121.

82 McGavran, *Understanding Church Growth*, 168.

83 *Ibid.*

84 Jo H. Lewis and Gordon A. Palmer, *What Every Christian Should Know*, 15.

85 *Ibid.*, 74.

86 Dudley and Cummings, 32.

87 Bellah, 143.

88 Michael Green, *Freed to Serve: Training and Equipping for Ministry*, 124.

89 Ellen G. White, *Evangelism*, 334.

90 Dudley and Cummings, 33.

91 Stott, 118.

92 White, *Evangelism*, 334.

93 Michael Green, *Evangelism in the Early Church*, 154.

94 *Ibid.*

95 *Ibid.*

96 Herb Miller, *Evangelism's Open Secrets*, 40.

97 Wagner, *Church Growth and the Whole Gospel*, 140.

98 *Ibid.*

99 *Ibid.*

100 George G. Hunter, III, *The Contagious Congregation*, 143.

101 George Gallup, Jr., and David Poling, *The Search for America's Faith*, 42-43.

102 Richard John Neuhaus, *Freedom for Ministry*, 101.

103 Michael Harper, *Let My People Grow*, 152.

104 Bill Hull, *Jesus Christ Disciplemaker*, 10.

105 Engel and Norton, 55.

106 George G. Hunter, III, 143. He suggests starting with very basic content for new believers, "sparing" none from receiving this instruction: Ten Commandments, Lord's Prayer, Apostles Creed; general introduction to the Bible plus concentration on one or two books (Luke, Galatians) and an introduction to the church and the mission of Christian lay people.

107 C. Peter Wagner, *Your Church Can Grow*, 111-126. Concept introduced and developed in his book is referenced here.

108 Tom Stebbins, *Evangelism by the Book*, 45.

109 See Hunter, 143.

110 Win Arn and Charles Arn, *The Master's Plan for Making Disciples*, 145-153.

111 Jard DeVille, *The Psychology of Witnessing*, 36-41. (Available from the General Conference Ministerial Association Resource Center. 301-680-6508; Fax: 301-680-6502.)

112 David Watson, *Called and Committed: World-Changing Discipleship*, 1982.

113 Alice Fryling, *Disciplemaker's Handbook.*

114 C. Peter Wagner, *Strategies for Church Growth*, 117-128.

115 Delbert Baker, V. Bailey Gillespie, and Alayne Thorpe, eds., *Welcome to the Family.*

116 Ervin R. Stutzman, *Welcome! A Biblical and Practical Guide to Receiving New Members.*

117 Herb Miller, *How to Build a Magnetic Church*, 86.

118 Michael Green, *To Corinth with Love*, 55.

119 John S. Savage, *The Apathetic and Bored Church Member*, 57.

120 Ken Abraham, *The Disillusioned Christian*, 127.

121 Peter Wagner's term to describe leaders–pastoral or laity–who see the world as Jesus sees it–full of potential subjects for His kingdom! They learn to value people the way heaven values people. They measure people by their potential

as servants of the King more than by their current station in life. They view the lost through "church growth eyes"!

122 C. Peter Wagner, *Leading Your Church to Growth,* 22-23.

123 *Ibid.,* 23-24.

124 Bailey E. Smith, *Real Evangelism,* 121.

125 Nelson Annan, *More People! Is Church Growth Worth It?*

126 Smith, 123.

127 R. Paul Stevens, *Liberating the Laity,* 33.

128 Stebbins, 218.

129 In Bellah, 131.

130 In Harvie M. Conn, *Evangelism: Doing Justice and Preaching Grace,* 29-30.

131 Cook and Baldwin, 11.

132 Conn, 29.

133 Robert Tuttle, Jr., *Someone Out There Needs Me,* 103.

134 Cook and Baldwin, 15.

135 *Ibid.,* 21.

136 *Ibid.,* 12.

137 See Flavil Yeakley, "A Profile of the New Convert: Change in Life Situation," in Win Arn, ed., *The Pastor's Church Growth Handbook,* 2:31.

138 Kent R. Hunter, *Foundations for Church Growth,* 155.

139 In Win Arn, "The Friendship Factor," *The Pastor's Church Growth Handbook,* 2:179.

140 In *Ibid.*

141 Ken Abraham, *The Disillusioned Christian,* 127.

142 Annan, 37-40. Emphasis mine.

143 Lyle E. Schaller, *Assimilating New Members,* 76-77.

144 Barna, *User Friendly Churches,* 94.

145 Tuttle, 125.

146 E. Glenn Hinson, *The Church: Design for Survival,* 95.

147 Kenneth L. Cober, *The Church's Teaching Ministry,* 31.

148 Rex D. Edwards, *A New Frontier: Every Believer a Minister,* 98.

149 In *Ibid.,* 97-98.

150 In Tuttle, 103.

151 *Ibid.*

152 Edwards, 98.

153 *Ibid.,* 100.

154 McGavran and Arn, 108.

155 Fannie L. Houck, *Beyond Baptism,* 9. Emphasis mine.

156 Stott, 121.

157 George Barna, *What Americans Believe,* 68-76.

158 Thompson, 156, 162.

159 Win Arn, ed., *The Pastor's Church Growth*

Handbook, 2:95-109. Emphasis mine.

160 Donald McGavran and George G. Hunter, III, *Church Growth: Strategies that Work,* 79-80.

161 Hadidian, 81.

162 Alvin J. Lindgren and Norman Shawchuck, *Let My People Go: Empowering Laity for Ministry,* 22.

163 Annan, 46.

164 Dudley and Cummings, 32.

165 In Win Arn, ed., *The Pastor's Church Growth Handbook,* 1:188.

166 Lyle E. Schaller, *Activating the Passive Church: Diagnosis and Treatment,* 122.

167 *Ibid.*

168 Calvin Ratz, Frank Tillapaugh, and Myron Augsburger, *Mastering Outreach and Evangelism,* 68.

169 Barna, *User Friendly Churches,* 114.

170 F. F. Bruce, *Paul and His Converts,* 28-29.

171 Douglas W. Johnson, *The Care and Feeding of Volunteers,* 35-53.

172 C. Kirk Hadaway, *What Can We Do About Church Dropouts?*

173 Keith Bailey, *Care of Converts.*

174 *Ibid.,* 7.

175 Gary McIntosh and Glen Martin, *Finding Them, Keeping Them: Effective Strategies for Evangelism and Assimilation in the Local Church.*

176 *Ibid.,* 75-135.

177 Max E. Anders, *30 Days to Understanding the Christian Life.*

178 *Ibid.,* 225.

179 *Ibid.,* 265.

180 George Barna, *The Frog in the Kettle,* 33.

181 *Ibid.,* 34.

182 In Anne Davis and Wade Rowatt, Jr., eds., *Formation for Christian Ministry,* 155-157.

183 Moeller, *1990 Cobb County (Georgia) Data Report.*

184 *Ibid.*

185 Congregational Survey (See Chapter 7).

186 Moeller, 9.

187 *Ibid.*

188 Rick Warren, *The Purpose Driven Church,* 156.

189 *Ibid.,* 157.

190 *Ibid.,* 158-159.

191 *Ibid.,* 160.

192 *Ibid.,* 170.

193 *Ibid.,* 171-172.

194 Lyle E. Schaller, "Denominational or Independent? Where are the Advantages?" *The Clergy Journal,* (August 1996), 20.

195 *Ibid.,* 21.

196 Ellen G. White, *Christ's Object Lessons,* 333.

Assignments for Spiritual Friends and "Do's and Don'ts"

Assignments for spiritual friends

Special Friend assignments are to be completed in order. Report each assignment when completed. Thank you!

___1. Visit the new member's home and introduce yourself as a special friend. Express your love and personal happiness for his/her membership in the Seventh-day Adventist church. *Give a copy of devotional book,* explaining that it gives a verse of scripture and a special devotional thought for each day and is a wonderful way to begin enjoying personal or family devotions on a daily basis. If appropriate, pray a short prayer and leave on a happy note: "I'll look forward to seeing you in church this Sabbath." *Important: maximum time for first visit is 5 minutes.*

___2. Visit new member's home and give them a *current church bulletin.* Explain that news items about the local church family will be listed in the bulletin along with the order of worship service, etc. Show them features such as other church services and activities, TV/radio programs sponsored by the church, etc.

___3. Choose one of the following options:
   a. Invite the new member to your home for Sabbath dinner.
   b. Invite the new member to join you at a church fellowship dinner.
   c. Invite the new member to eat Sabbath dinner with you in a picnic/ park setting.

___4. Visit new member's homes and give them a current copy of *Signs of the Times* magazine. Explain that this is a monthly prophecy journal published by the Adventist church for the general public and that *you have already ordered a year's subscription for them.* Note: This may have been done through the conference office.

___5. Introduce the new member to another church member whom they have not already met. It is especially appropriate to do this at a church service. Just say, "I want you to meet someone I think you will enjoy knowing." Do not leave these two new acquaintances awkwardly fumbling for conversation.

___6. Choose one of the following options:
   a. Invite the new member to your home for a meal.
   b. Share a hobby, recreational activity, shopping trip, etc. with new member.
   c. Take a gift of food (fruit, cookies, bread, etc.) to the new member's home.

___7. Visit the new member at home, giving a current copy of the *Sabbath School Study Guide.* Explain how each lesson is divided into a short segment for daily study. Show how each question is *always answered with a Bible text* and that additional materials for background and commentary are often provided. Encourage the new member to continue attending the Pastor's

Bible Class for the present time, but recommend that they will enjoy daily study from the study guide.

___8. Choose one of the following options:

    a. Take the new member to visit the church school, academy, Adventist hospital, or college that is nearest you. Try to go while the students are in class if it is a school day.

    b. Take the new member with you to the Adventist Book Center.

    c. Provide some service of kindness, babysitting, or running an errand for the new member. *Show that you care!*

___9. Visit the new member's home and give them a current copy of the *Adventist Review* and the local union paper. Explain that this weekly magazine is for all church members and that it is the worldwide journal for Adventist Christians. Show them the various features. Also explain that the union paper gives articles and reports about the work of God's church in our region of the nation. Show them the section for our conference. Isn't it wonderful to belong to a worldwide church? Order a year's subscription of the *Adventist Review* as your gift to the new member.

___10. Visit the new member and explain what camp meeting is all about. Tell them when it is conducted in your conference and invite them to plan to go with you for the entire week—or at least the weekends.

___11. Choose one of the following options:

    a. Invite the new member to your home for a meal.

    b. Share a hobby, recreational activity, shopping trip, etc. with new member.

    c. Take a gift of food (cookies, pie, bread, fruit, etc.) to member.

___12. Visit new member's home and give a copy of *Bible Readings for the Home;* explain how to use it as an encyclopedia of Bible questions and topics.

___13. Choose one of the following options:

    a. Invite new member to your home for a meal.

    b. Introduce new member to another church member they have not met.

    c. Take the new member on a short trip to visit an Adventist institution.

___14. Visit new member and take a current copy of one of the following magazines: *Vibrant Life, Listen, Liberty.* Either subscribe for them or show them how to order a subscription.

___15. Choose one of the following options:

    a. Invite the new member to *participate with you* in some witnessing activity: literature distribution, ingathering, prayer or fellowship group, etc.

    b. Invite the new member to attend or assist in a special school program, Quit Now, parenting class, cooking school, stress clinic, etc.

___16. Ask the new member to share with a Sabbath school class, or the entire congregation, what led them into membership in the Adventist church. As an alternative, ask the new member to present the scripture reading or another part of a church program. *Note:* Many individuals are uncomfortable praying in public, so request some other activity.

___17. Visit the new member and tell them about *Breath of Life, Faith for Today, It Is Written, La Voz de la Esperanza, Voice of Prophecy,* or *Amazing Facts and the Quiet Hour,* etc. Emphasize that these programs are all sponsored by the Adventist church and write down a list of those that appear in your area along with the stations and times.

___18. Visit the new member's home, taking a copy of *Desire of Ages.* Explain that this is the best one-volume life of Christ available. *Notice: this is not a visit to discuss the doctrine of the spirit of prophecy.* If this becomes necessary, contact your pastor.

___19. Choose one of the following options:
   a. Invite new member to share with you in visiting a sick member, shut-in, etc.
   b. Invite new member to share a talent they might have with your church family.
   c. Introduce new member to another church member they may not have met.

___20. Invite the new member to assist you in enrolling some other person in Bible studies. Get them involved in going with you to a series of studies. If it is appropriate, let them lead the study, but you should always be there to guide each study session.

___21. Invite the new member to visit one of the children's Sabbath school classes, a session of the Pathfinder Club, the local church school, the conference youth camp, or the conference academy. Demonstrate what Adventists are doing for our young people.

___22. Share the book of the year with the new member and, if possible, invite them to go with you to visit the Adventist Book Center.

___23. Choose one of the following options:
   a. Invite the new member to your home for a meal.
   b. Share a hobby, recreational activity, shopping trip, etc. with new member.
   c. Take a gift of food to new member's home.

___24. Share with your pastor your personal evaluation of this process along with your suggestions for improving the new member assimilation process.

Some suggestions for special friends: do's and don'ts
1. *Do* love this soul for whom Jesus died. Verbally express your love and friendship.
2. *Do* complete each assignment in sequence. Make it your week's goal to complete the project.
3. *Do* mail your assignment card to the office as soon as the project is done.
4. *Do* call the pastor regarding any question that might arise. Simply say, "Let's ask the pastor." Then, make a point to ask the pastor!
5. *Do* seek and greet your new member at all church services and programs.
6. *Do* look for ways to involve the new member in church projects, programs, and activities. Introduce the new member to other members and church leaders.

7. *Do* make frequent verbal reports to the Assimilation Committee concerning the progress of the new member.

8. *Do* verbally express your love to the new member often.

9. *Do* visit your new member at home if possible. Better yet, invite them to your home. Remember, make *only short* visits!

10. *Do* speak in only positive terms regarding the church, the conference, other members, the pastors, etc.

11. *Do* conclude each visit on a happy note. Make new members glad they know you and glad they are members of your church.

12. *Don't* answer doctrinal questions. You are their friend, not their instructor.

13. *Don't* preach or give advice. Your role is that of special friend, not elder, pastor, or advisor.

14. *Don't* let two weeks pass without contacting your new member.

15. *Don't* be shocked at a new member's suggestions (i.e., television on Sabbath, cup of coffee, etc.). They have been thoroughly prepared for church membership but may forget or still be growing in spiritual maturity.

16. *Don't* act superior or condescending because you have been a member longer.

17. *Don't* give extra reading material above that which is listed. If you feel a particular book is needed, contact the pastor and ask him to present it.

18. *Don't* tell the new member that you are assigned to "check up" on them.

19. *Don't* tell the new member that you give a weekly report to the Assimilation Committee.

20. *Don't* share church gossip or problems with the new member.

21. *Don't* downgrade other denominations. If they mention another church, simply say, *"There are many wonderful people there!"*

22. *Don't* let the new member see your assignment sheet or response cards. Make your projects seem as spontaneous as possible.

Appendix B

Following are samples of various weekly letters sent from the pastor to all new members. These are given here in the order they were sent, but you will need to adapt them for your own local area. The purpose of these letters is to review basic doctrinal and church polity information as an ongoing orientation process for new believers. Letters should be written on church letterhead and personally addressed and signed.

Letter 1

Dear Friend:

How thankful we are to the Lord Jesus, our Saviour, for your membership in the wonderful Seventh-day Adventist family!

What a privilege to be waiting for Jesus to return and to ask the Holy Spirit to aid each of us in sharing this good news of the gospel with those we meet.

We have come to love you and want to assure you that you are always in our prayers. Also we request that you remember us in prayer to the Saviour. We know how important it is that the Holy Spirit be in our lives and that we allow His influence to speak through our work.

As a new believer, you will find your spiritual life will grow as you apply the following principles in your personal life: Bible Study, Prayer, Fellowship, Witnessing, and Obedience.

I will cover each of these in greater depth in future letters and show you how to grow personally in your relationship to Jesus Christ in these important areas.

Again, please remember that we are praying for you.

Your friend in our Saviour's service,

Letter 2

Dear Friend:

When I last wrote you, I encouraged you to look at five principles for a growing experience with Jesus: Bible Study, Prayer, Fellowship, Witnessing, and Obedience.

Knowledge of God's plan for your personal life is essential for your spiritual growth. The way to learn more about God is to study His Word. Daily study of the Bible builds a strong foundation for future spiritual progress.

If you are not a regular Bible reader, begin with something simple like the Gospel of Luke in the New Testament or Genesis, the first book of the Bible. In the stories of the Bible, look for people who have situations similar to your own. Think about how God treated them or how Jesus personally related to those to whom He ministered.

If you already read the Bible regularly, one helpful way to grow spiritually is to add just ten minutes per day to what you are currently doing. If you currently read God's Word for ten minutes each day, try expanding your time to twenty minutes. You will find spiritual strength comes by increased contact with Scripture. After a few weeks, try to expand your time another ten minutes per day. If you don't currently read the Bible consistently, then try starting with just ten minutes per day.

It is always appropriate to begin your personal devotions with a prayer. Ask the Holy Spirit to teach you from God's Word. The very best prayer could be your heartfelt request, "Lord, show me Your will for my life."

I am very interested in your progress in reading from God's Word. Please let me know if you need additional help and how your intentions are progressing into reality.

I am praying for you as you go deeper into the Scripture.

Your friend in our Saviour's service,

Letter 3

Dear Friend:

You are being prayed for every day. Our intercessory prayer group keeps a list of our new members and lifts your name before our Heavenly Father on a daily basis. Likewise, I am praying for you and I ask that you also remember me in your prayers.

One Christian writer says it well: "Prayer is the opening of our heart to God as to a friend." Prayer is a blessing not only to us as we pray but also to those for whom we pray. It is a real privilege to lift up our joys, needs, and petitions in prayer to Jesus.

The New Testament book of Hebrews says Jesus, our High Priest, hears and answers our prayers. Jesus understands our weaknesses and is ready to give us strength and sends the Holy Spirit to aid us. Many people say they don't understand how to pray and get answers. Let me share with you a simple process.

ASK: Jesus says, "Ask and it shall be given you" (Matthew 7:7). What shall I ask for? Ask what God has promised in the Bible. Did you know that the Bible contains thousands of promises and God invites you to ask for His promised blessings? One of my favorite promises is "In all thy ways acknowledge Him, and He shall direct thy paths." Notice the promise! God will personally direct our path through life. What a blessing. Notice also, there is a condition to the promise. I must acknowledge God in my life. What good would His guidance be to me if I would not permit Him to control my life? Do you see? Ask according to what God has promised in His Word, the Bible.

BELIEVE: Jesus says, "What things soever ye desire, when ye pray, believe that you receive them, and ye shall have them" (Mark 11:24). Why ask God for His promised blessings if you don't believe you will receive them? God's power is given to us as we believe!

CLAIM: Claim the promised blessing for your own life by thanking God that you have received it. You may not yet see the answer, but you have God's promise that He will indeed answer. You may not know the end from the beginning, but God has promised that "all things work together for good to them that love Him and who are called according to His purpose." So thank the Saviour for hearing and answering your prayer. This is *claiming* the promise just like Jesus did at Lazarus' tomb. Notice, Lazarus was still dead, but Jesus said, "Father, I thank Thee that Thou hast heard me."

As you begin to use these simple ABCs of Bible prayer, you will experience the full joy of knowing that Jesus will help you in all your daily activities and problems.

Your friend in our Saviour's service,

Letter 4

Dear Friend:

Fellowship is one of the five essential building blocks of a growing relationship with Jesus.

The apostle Paul puts it this way: *"Not forsaking the assembling of ourselves together, as the manner of some is; but exhorting one another; and so much the more, as ye see the day approaching"* (Hebrews 10:15).

Notice what Paul is saying. As we see "the day when Jesus will return" approaching, we need more than ever the strength we get from assembling together to worship and study God's Word.

Sometimes we think that perhaps we can grow in Jesus just as quickly if we stay at home and worship there rather than attending worship services on Sabbath.

Now, of course, if a person is ill, then he or she can commune with the Saviour at home on the Lord's Day. However, when we have our health, we need to take every opportunity for fellowship together.

Not only does the worship service strengthen us personally, but it also strengthens others who need their faith lifted. That is what Paul means when he says "exhorting one another." Your attendance at the worship service may do someone else as much good, through your personal example, as it does for you.

Naturally Satan would do everything possible to weaken our resolve to follow Jesus and His wonderful truth. If he can keep me home from church week after week, then Satan has gained a very real victory. However, if we are worshiping the Saviour each Lord's Day in the joy of Jesus, then we are victorious over the devil through the power of the Holy Spirit.

We are praying for you every day. It is our prayer that you are attending the worship services regularly each Sabbath and receiving a blessing from worshiping Jesus.

Your friend in our Saviour's service,

Letter 5

Dear Friend:

What a privilege it is to be looking forward to the soon return of Jesus. Our Saviour says in the book of Revelation, *"Behold I come quickly."* How we long for that day when Jesus returns.

As we look forward to Jesus' return, it is also a joy to remember that because He died on Calvary's cross for our sins, we can have the assurance of salvation through faith in His shed blood.

The joy of our salvation, however, also brings privileged responsibility. As we live for Jesus we are witnesses to others of the power of the Saviour in our lives. In fact, our lives may be the only sermons some people will ever hear. How does my life represent the saving love of Jesus? This is a question I often ask. Am I showing that I really am looking forward to His second coming?

Personally, I can't think of a better way to effectively witness to others about the love of Jesus than to be a genuine friend who is interested in their lives and activities. This is the way that Jesus reached people. He was interested in them.

Perhaps you know of some friend or relative with whom you want to share some of the wonderful truths you have been learning as you have become a part of the Seventh-day Adventist church. Try being a real, concerned, and loving friend—doing a good deed, speaking a loving word, sharing a chore—and then invite your friend or relative to attend a worship service with you.

Actually, you have opportunities to reach the lives of individuals who would never come to hear the sermons of any pastor. Yet, as they see that Jesus is living in you and that you are happy in His love, they will want to know this marvelous Saviour.

Witnessing for Jesus is an essential part of growing strong in your relationship with God. Remember, we are praying for you and asking that the Holy Spirit will continue to give you strength.

Your friend in our Saviour's service,

Letter 6

Dear Friend:

Sometimes people are a little confused. Perhaps you have mentioned to someone that you are worshiping on the Lord's Day Saturday Sabbath, and they have responded, "But hasn't the Sabbath commandment been done away with?" Or perhaps someone has said, "Oh, we are saved by grace. We don't need to obey the Ten Commandments."

Let me share just two texts that have helped me understand these questions: The first is Ephesians 2:8-10. "For by grace are ye saved through faith; and that not of yourselves; it is the gift of God: Not of works, lest any man should boast. For we are His workmanship, created in Christ Jesus unto good works, which God hath before ordained that we should walk in them."

Of course we are saved by grace and grace alone. No person will ever be in the kingdom of heaven by his own good works. No person will ever be saved by what day he or she keeps holy. However, Paul points out in this text that an individual who is "saved by grace" is "created in Christ Jesus unto good works."

A person is not created in Christ Jesus unto evil works or sin. The Bible says that sin is the transgression of God's law. I cannot be loving Jesus fully if I am willfully breaking one of His commandments. In fact, Jesus says, "If ye love me, keep my commandments" (John 14:15). Notice, *if you love Jesus,* then consequentially you will want to obey Him! The Sabbath commandment is not different from the other nine.

The second text, Romans 6:14-15, puts it this way: "For sin shall not have dominion over you; for ye are not under the law, but under grace. What then? Shall we sin, because we are not under the law, but under grace? God forbid!" Paul says that we must never conclude that the saving grace of Jesus gives us a license to live for the devil. No! God forbid!

The person who is saved by grace will want the Holy Spirit to help him follow as Jesus leads! Sin is breaking God's law. The Sabbath is part of God's law. And Paul in the New Testament tells us that when we are saved by grace we will want to follow Jesus in obedience.

This is not salvation by works at all! It is following Jesus because He has saved us by His matchless grace

What a privilege to follow as Jesus leads us. Obedience to Jesus is never the method of obtaining salvation. It is always a fruit of our relationship with the Saviour!

Your friend in our Saviour's service,

Letter 7

Dear Friend:

I want to share with you a blessing that I have found in the Seventh-day Adventist church family that will also be of tremendous help in your own life. I am speaking of the Sabbath School study hour each Saturday morning.

As you already know, each Sabbath we have a Sabbath School program and classes in addition to the worship service. This is a special opportunity for growing in the love of Jesus as we study God's Word together.

Perhaps you have already found a particular class which you are enjoying. However, if you have not yet experienced one of the classes, may we suggest that this very next Sabbath you make it a point to attend the Sabbath School program and sit in on one of the classes to enjoy the discussion.

Usually the Sabbath School program features a special "mission report" which tells of the power of the Holy Spirit working throughout the world. This is a worldwide message to help everyone prepare to meet Jesus, and how encouraging it is to hear these wonderful reports of the work of God's people around the globe. In fact, Seventh-day Adventists believe so strongly in a worldwide mission program that each Sabbath an offering is received which goes directly to the expansion of these great mission projects. This offering goes only for mission work. Thus we can share in proclaiming the gospel around the world, although we may never leave our homes!

In the classes each person is given an opportunity to discuss the lesson which all have studied from the *Sabbath School Study Guide*. Of course no one is forced to talk or answer questions. You may wish to volunteer a comment or to read a text of Scripture.

I have found great strength in discussing specific Bible topics with other Christians in the Sabbath School class. I hope you will begin right away enjoying Sabbath School if you have not already attended. I know it will be a source of strength to you.

Your friend in our Saviour's service,

Letter 8

Dear Friend:

This is to share with you the fact that soon you will be receiving three wonderful and encouraging magazines by mail. These will be coming to your home free of charge as a gift from your church family as we rejoice in your being a member of our congregation.

My spouse and I receive each of these journals in our own home, and they mean a great deal to us. Let me briefly describe them to you:

Adventist Review—This weekly magazine is our worldwide general church paper. It contains inspirational articles, editorials, studies on prophecies, and important Biblical topics. It also brings reports of the activities, programs, and evangelistic outreaches of the church all around the globe. The annual subscription rate is about $40, but this magazine comes to you for a full year as a *free gift*. As far as we are concerned, this is the most important journal we receive in our home. We know it will be a source of enjoyment and inspiration to you and it will inform you of our church's global ministry.

Signs of the Times—This monthly journal presents the full gospel message in its pages. It is beautifully illustrated and contains articles on Bible prophecies and important subjects from Scripture. Again, this will come to your home for one year as a free gift from your church family. *Signs* is published by Pacific Press in Nampa, Idaho, one of many publishing companies owned and staffed by dedicated Seventh-day Adventist Christians. We know that you will find this magazine a real blessing.

Southern Tidings—This monthly journal comes free to the home of every member in the states of North and South Carolina, Georgia, Florida, Alabama, Mississippi, Tennessee, and Kentucky. Its purpose is to give you a report of the activities of local congregations throughout this area. You will be encouraged as you see the progress of God's work and wonderful truth right here in our own part of the nation. It is very likely you may even see reports of the activities of your own church family in its pages.

In closing, let me again stress the need for your continued search for spiritual strength and fellowship which comes not only through Bible study and your continued prayers, but also by your attendance and participation in church activities. Your friend in our Saviour's service,

Letter 9
Dear Friend:

Perhaps you have wondered how the Adventist church is organized. I would like to briefly outline the structure for your understanding. As you begin to see that this is a worldwide message to prepare everyone for the soon return of Jesus, you will join me in thanking the Holy Spirit for an organized movement of people who proclaim Jesus' love and Bible truth.

General Conference of Seventh-day Adventists—The world headquarters of the Adventist church is in Silver Spring, Maryland, near Washington, D.C. The "GC" is divided into a dozen divisions which usually include several nations per division. Pastor Jan Paulsen is the world leader of the Adventist church. The General Conference, through its twelve divisions, is known around the world for humanitarian, evangelistic, and educational work. The North American Division is also headquartered in Silver Spring. *You are a member of the General Conference of Seventh-day Adventists through its North American Division.*

Southern Union Conference of Seventh-day Adventists. World divisions of the "GC" are divided into regional unions, nine in North America. Atlanta is the headquarters for the southern United States. This union's projects include Southern Adventist University, a fully-accredited four-year liberal arts university near Chattanooga, Tennessee; numerous community hospitals throughout these states; distribution of books through the work of literature evangelists; and many other areas of outreach including youth ministry, evangelism, children's ministries, and community service/disaster relief programs. The Southern Union is divided into eight local conferences. *You are a member of the Southern Union of Seventh-day Adventists.*

The Local Conference of Seventh-day Adventists. The work of the Adventist family in closer areas comes under the direction of the conference—usually comprising the same boundaries as state lines, although sometimes states may be combined into one conference or a large state may have several conferences within its territory. Among the many projects of the local conferences are senior high schools (academies) and numerous elementary schools where our young people can learn about Jesus while receiving an outstanding education.

The local conferences also show interest in young people by providing beautiful camps where youngsters spend summer weeks learning of the love of the Saviour along with the wonders of nature. Evangelistic outreach programs are an integral part of the local conference, which may coordinate bringing evangelistic crusades to various areas in each conference's territory. Community service centers throughout the conferences give free diagnostic health screenings and provide instant emergency relief at the time of tornadoes, floods, fires, and other disasters. The Georgia-Cumberland Conference is made up of congregations throughout Georgia and East Tennessee. *You are a member of the Georgia-Cumberland Conference of Seventh-day Adventists.*

Your Local Congregation is one of the many throughout the world (nearly 5,000 in North America) ranging in size from the smallest of about five members in a tiny hamlet to the largest of around 5,000 members in major areas. However, the average church membership is around 75-100 members who are working together to share in the proclamation of the joyous return of Jesus.

Among the activities you will find in your local congregation are welfare and community service programs, Pathfindering (like scouting) for youngsters, stop smoking plans, volunteer service projects, and often a local elementary school offering high-quality education coupled with a deeply spiritual atmosphere.

Local church officers are elected for one- or two-year terms, usually in the fall of the year. Every church member has a vote. The individuals for church office are presented to the church family by a nominating committee which has previously been selected by the members themselves. Church officers are responsible for the various activities and projects for the local congregation during their term of service.

Your pastor is appointed by the local Conference Committee to serve the congregation. Your tithe does not stay with the local pastor but goes to the world headquarters of the church, through your conference, to help spread the gospel throughout the world. *You are a member of the Marietta Seventh-day Adventist Church.*

Now that you have this brief overview of the various church activities and organization, have you discovered who the most important individual in the church is? It is not the pastor, not the local conference president, not even the world leader of our church. *It is you! That's right—it is you!* You see, as we work together in our local churches for Jesus, our wonderful Saviour, we can hasten that glad day when He will come.

Since it is up to you and me, then you can quickly see we must cooperate and work together to tell everyone of Jesus' love. The soon return of Jesus is what Sharon and I long for. It is our prayer that you will strongly support all the activities of your church so that we can share together in proclaiming the Bible truth for today!

We are praying for you.

Your friend in our Saviour's service,

Letter 10

Dear Friend:

Among other things you may hear discussed in an Adventist church is a term that may be unfamiliar to you. I want to share briefly with you this important item, for it will be a real blessing to your own life.

Camp Meeting—camp meeting, or "camp" as it is sometimes described, is a term which describes a great series of spiritual meetings which takes place each year—usually sometime during the summer months. Seventh-day Adventist Christians from all over the conference come together for a full week of Bible study, practical instructional classes, inspirational preaching, and some of the most marvelous music this side of heaven.

Where does everybody stay? That is why it's called "camp" meeting! First there are usually dormitories on the academy (boarding high school) or college campus where camp meetings are often held and these dorm rooms are available for those attending the camp meeting. Then, hundreds of Christians use family-size tents or individual campers, trailers, motor homes, etc. And a few brave individuals, usually younger folk, even camp right out under the stars. Others stay in motels nearby.

Meetings typically start early each morning and go right through the day, concluding with a preaching service in the evening. Naturally everyone breaks for meals which are either prepared in the tents or trailers or purchased at the full-service cafeterias which are also on campus. You are not required to attend every meeting. In fact, you will probably have a difficult time choosing which of the various options you will squeeze into your schedule. However, I can promise you from personal experience that whatever portion of the camp meeting you can attend will return to you wonderful blessings.

Many members are able to come to camp meeting only for the weekends (camp meetings usually start on Friday evening and continue for a full week, concluding the next Saturday night). However, hundreds of Adventist Christians tell me they schedule their vacations so they can attend the full week of camp meeting.

When camp meeting times comes again, I hope you will join the thousands of other Christians who will receive a blessing by experiencing the wonderful things which are provided.

We are praying for you every day!
Your friend in our Saviour's service,

Letter 11

Dear Friend:

Someone recently asked me a question which I thought was of general interest and thus I am writing each of our members. The question was, "What happens to the money I give to the church on Sabbath morning?"

Of course you understand the Bible principle of tithing—returning to the Lord one tenth of our increase. The Bible speaks of this tenth plus our offerings in many passages, including Malachi 3:8-12. The Bible also points out that the tithe is to be used to support the preaching of the gospel message to all the world.

Your pastor does not keep the tithe money which is turned in each Sabbath. In fact, not one bit of the tithe money ever remains with the local church. There are some areas of the world where the local congregations cannot earn enough money to even support the missionaries and ministers who serve them. Therefore, all the tithe is forwarded, through the conference, to our world headquarters where it is then distributed throughout the world to support the preaching of the gospel.

Some of the tithe remains in the local conference from where your pastors receive their salary. Through their tithe, Adventists in North America, who are blessed so abundantly, support much of the church's work in many other nations where living conditions and earning capacities are much lower than our standard of living. So you see, as I personally return my tithe to Jesus, I may have a part in preaching the gospel to all the world even though I may never get to preach in other lands.

Another area of giving is our offerings. These are usually divided into two categories—*local offerings* and *conference offerings*. You can easily distinguish these two areas on your giving envelope. Conference offerings are used to support evangelistic meetings throughout your state, the educational system, and many other fine programs such as youth evangelism, community service projects, etc.

Local offerings support the upkeep and activities of the local congregation. The money turned in for these areas stays in the local church to pay utility bills, pay repair and maintenance bills, and fund other local projects such as Vacation Bible School, community services, and other local programs.

As you can see, there are many worthy projects in which we can share. The overall principle of stewardship with Jesus is consistent faithfulness. It isn't only how much a person gives but what the condition of our heart is! "God loves a cheerful giver."
Your friend in our Saviour's service,

Letter 12
Dear Friend:

This is the last of our orientation letters for new members which you will be receiving. It hardly seems possible that three months have passed since you first became part of our congregation.

Of course you will still receive our weekly newsletter and other items that I send to all the members, but I have always believed that some extra information is useful as you become a member of our church family. I hope you have found these letters helpful and informative. I would personally welcome your suggestions as to how this program can better serve the needs of newcomers in our church.

Please remember the essentials that you've heard me talk about so much: Bible Study, Prayer, Fellowship, Witnessing, and Obedience.

These are the essential elements of spiritual growth and a continually growing relationship with Jesus Christ.

Again, special blessings to you every day. You remain in my prayers.
Your friend in our Saviour's service!

Appendix C

Love Feast

Joseph and Gwendolyn Coleman

*Joseph and Gwendolyn Coleman are active lay members of Dupont Park
Seventh-day Adventist Church, Washington, D.C. who because of their concern
about the "revolving door" syndrome created the Love Feast Ministry.*

1. *Love Feast:* **What it Is**

Love Feast is a program designed to help newly baptized and transferred
members feel welcome, comfortable, and accepted. It gives the entire church body
an opportunity to extend love to these members as they get settled in *their* new
church home. Special features of the program are *Get Acquainted* Sabbath
dinners, *Welcome Wagon* dinners, socials, and the *Love Feast Program Connection.*

The *Love Feast Program* is directed by a chairperson who selects officers and
assistants such as: secretary, historian, photographer, etc.

The chairperson works closely with the pastor, assistant pastor, first elder,
and Bible instructor—keeping them abreast of any special needs or special areas
of concern that may merit their personal attention. A letter explaining the *Love
Feast Program* is sent to each church board member *(see sample letter 1a).*

The program aims to encourage every church member to become actively
involved with the nurturing of new members. The "epistle" and volunteer form
(see samples 1b and 1c) may be helpful in bringing the program to the attention of
your church family.

Sample 1a: Letter to church board members

Date:

Dear Church Board Member:

The Love Feast Program Committee would like to provide you an overview
and show you the many benefits this program brings to all involved. The *Love
Feast* is an organization formed primarily to welcome new members into the
church family. Transition from one church to another is not easy; people choose
their home churches based on their feelings of acceptance. Through a series of
welcome activities, those involved in the *Love Feast Program* endeavor to make
new members feel loved and accepted early in their relationship with the church.

Love Feast Program activities are held at least once a quarter for all new
members accepted into the church during the previous quarter. The following
activities should be systematically planned.

1. The *Love Feast* chairperson or first elder invites new members to his/her
    home to a *Get Acquainted* Sabbath dinner. The new members are greeted
    by committee members and enjoy warmth, good food, and fellowship. After
    dinner, each new member offers testimony and is encouraged to ask
    questions. This dinner helps promote the family-like environment that
    the *Love Feast Program* hopes to engender.

2. New members then receive a formal invitation to their own *Love Feast*, an event held in the church dining hall. Homemade breads, seasonal fruit, nuts, and fruit juices are served. New members have their own reserved table, are presented their baptismal certificates or transfer certificates, and are extended the right hand of fellowship by the church members in attendance. A member of the Nurturing Committee will present each attendee with "love gifts" such as spiritual books and sunset calenders. Through interaction with the new members, this committee also determines in which areas of church ministry the new members would like to participate.

3. Shortly thereafter, the new members are "enrolled" in the *Welcome Wagon*. This committee consists of a group of host families who extend invitations to the new members for Sabbath dinner and fellowship. These committee members agree to hold fellowship dinners for a one-year term. This is an excellent way to make new members feel like part of the church family.

4. *Love Feast* socials and picnics are planned for all members. Food, fun, and games are great ways to participate in Christian entertainment and fellowship.

5. New members are contacted by the members of the *Love Feast Connection*, a group of people who share information and cheerful greetings over the phone.

All church board members are encouraged to look at the pictorial poster located in the church lobby. This features the new members' pictures and will be updated each quarter. Please seek these people out and greet them warmly.

The *Love Feast* is hosted by you, the board member, and alternating Sabbath School classes. Each quarter the *Love Feast* secretary will send you a request form listing a food item. Please be responsible for furnishing that item for the *Love Feast* banquet. We are happy to invite you to join the *Love Feast* but ask that you *please* adhere to the RSVP due to the limited amount of space we have in the church dining hall.

Please keep us in your prayers as the Lord continues to richly bless our effort.
Yours in Christ,
Love Feast Chairperson   *Love Feast* Secretary

Sample 1b: Epistle from the Love Feast Program

To the Congregation

The Lord has richly blessed our church family with many new members, but how many do you know? The *Love Feast Program* can aid you in getting acquainted with our new members. This program consists of a *Love Feast*, the *Welcome Wagon*, a *Social Committee*, and the *Love Feast Program Connection*. Each newly baptized member and transferred member is invited to participate.

You can become involved in helping our new members feel comfortable in their new church home and, at the same time, develop new friendships in Christ. If you wish to learn more about the program, please read the enclosed report and let us know where you think you can best serve. Place a check mark to indicate your area of interest. A program member will be at each exit of the church at the end of today's service to receive your response.

The Love Feast is held once a quarter. Fruits in season, nuts, homemade breads, and juices are served. Volunteers are needed to supply these items and to supply special music for the program.

The Welcome Wagon invites newly baptized and recently transferred members to their homes for dinner or social gatherings.

The Love Feast Program Connection keeps in contact with new members via the telephone.

The Social Committee plans Christian recreation and fellowship activities.

Sample 1c: The Love Feast Program volunteer form

I am interested in working in the following capacity/capacities:

_____ Love Feast   _____ Love Feast Program Connection

_____ Welcome Wagon   _____ Social Committee

Name: _____

Address: _____

City: _____ State: _____ Zip: _____

Telephone: Home (_____)   Work (_____)

2. Guidelines for *Love Feast*

Chairperson

The chairperson coordinates the following series of activities for newly baptized and recently transferred members.

1. Visits the baptismal class to get acquainted with the new believers. During this visit, each member is given a *Friendship Sheet* to complete *(see sample sheets 2a and 2b)*.
2. Invites newly baptized members to his/her or the elder's home for a *Get Acquainted* Sabbath dinner. They are greeted by *Love Feast Program* members and enjoy good food and fellowship. After dinner, each member is asked to offer a personal testimony. This dinner helps to instill the family-like environment the program hopes to engender.
3. Arranges and invites the new members to experience their very own love feast. The first one is usually held the quarter immediately following their baptism *(see sample 2c)*. This event is held in the church dining hall. Wholesome food is served. Each new member is seated at a reserved table that is shared with family and friends. Baptismal certificates and/or transfer certificates are presented, and the right hand of fellowship is extended by

the pastor and other church members in attendance. The Nurturing Committee presents each new member with a "love gift."

4. Arranges for the *Welcome Wagon Committee,* a group of host families, to invite new members for Sabbath dinner and fellowship. Each host family is asked to serve for one year.

5. Arranges for the Social Committee to hold *Love Feast* social activities (for example: food, fun, and games, or a picnic) at least twice during the year.

6. Ensures that the members of the *Love Feast Program Connection* keep in phone contact with new members.

Historian

The historian for the *Love Feast Program* collects the data presented on the *Friendship Sheets (see samples 2a and 2b)* and combines this data with photos taken during the program. This information is creatively placed in an album to be shared with the church family. At a glance you know the person's favorite song, Scripture, hobbies, etc.

A photo is also taken of each new and transferred member and placed in the church lobby or similar location for four to six weeks in order that the church family may become acquainted with names and faces.

The Love Feast

The Love Feast is one of the highlights of the program and is meant to make members feel very special. Newly baptized and/or recently transferred members, along with their families and friends, are invited to a special feast in their honor. Senior citizens and visitors may also be invited. The feast takes place after the divine worship hour *(see sample invitation 2C).*

To involve as many members of the church family as possible, the church board and Sabbath School classes are asked to supply the food served at the *Love Feast.* They also may attend the *Love Feasts* so they can become acquainted with new members.

Food served

The Love Feast is served with wholesome simplicity in mind. A typical meal may consist of the following: fruits—all kinds (including juices); grains—homemade breads; nuts—pecans, walnuts, peanuts; spreads—peanut butter, margarine, cream cheese. The food, arranged on the main serving table buffet style, gives an attractive and inviting appearance. Having youth hostesses and hosts serve the fruit juice to the guests individually adds a nice personal touch.

Two weeks before the *Love Feast,* a designated assistant to the chairperson visits the appointed Sabbath School class (more than one class may be used in order to accommodate the number of expected guests) and alerts them that their class has been selected to supply the provisions *(see sample 2d).* The secretary should send notes to the Board members to remind them of the upcoming event *(see sample note 2e).*

One week before the *Love Feast,* revisit the Sabbath School and assign each member, in writing, a particular food. Specify the time and place to deposit the food *(see sample 2f).* In order to be ready to greet guests immediately after the worship service, allow enough time between the receipt of the food, its preparation, setting tables, etc., before the time of the meal.

Hosts and hostesses should escort new members to a table that has been especially reserved for them. The blessing is given shortly after the guests arrive. They are escorted to the serving table while favorite hymns are being played.

Program

As the meal proceeds, present a short program. During the program, give each new member a baptismal certificate and/or a transfer certificate. Pastor and other members should extend the right hand of fellowship. Ask new members to give a short personal testimony of how they were introduced to the church. Afterwards, the Nurturing Committee presents "love gifts" to each.

Photos may be taken during the program to be included in an album by the historian as a pictorial history for future enjoyment. These pictures are also posted in a place where the entire church body can see them and begin to associate names with faces.

The program ends with everyone gathering in a large circle for singing and a concluding prayer *(see sample program 2g)*.

Love Feast Youth Hostess/Host Guidelines

The Hostess/Host Coordinator is responsible for contacting the hostesses/ hosts and their parents at least two weeks in advance of the upcoming *Love Feast*. The coordinator also reminds them again the night before. The coordinator is responsible for finding substitutes when necessary. Youth hostesses/hosts assist in table setting, serving senior guests, and assisting parents with small children.

All tables have a centerpiece (one basket of fresh fruit) and cups filled with nuts/raisins with a spoon in each.

One serving table is prepared for senior citizens. This table is a self-serve table with food already on it so guests are not required to get up unless they choose to. This table will have trays of bread, nuts, spreads, etc. Hostesses/hosts should be ready to assist as needed.

During the Love Feast program, the hostesses/hosts are to be stationed in various areas of the dining hall to serve guests as needed. Once everyone has been served, they can refill drinks and ice, serve second helpings, etc.

Once closing prayer has been offered, youth hostesses/hosts may distribute take-away bags to each table so guests may help themselves to any leftover food.

After the majority of guests have left the dining hall, the youth hostesses/ hosts help with the cleanup.

Sample 2a: Friendship Sheet

Seventh-day Adventist Church Love Feast
(Adult)

Newly Baptized _____   Date _____

Transfer _____

Male _____   Female _____

Name _____

Address _____

City _____ State _____ Zip _____

Phone Number _____   Birthday _____

Date of baptism _____   Date of transfer _____

Introduced to the church by _____

Marital status _____ Number of Children: _____ Girls _____ Boys _____

Hobbies _____

Favorite hymn or gospel song _____

Favorite Bible text _____

Would you like to have a spiritual partner assigned to you?   Yes_____ No _____

Are you interested in working in the church? Yes____ No ____ Perhaps in future ___

If yes, list your areas of interest:

   1.

   2.

Suggestions/comments:

Sample 2b: Friendship Sheet

**Seventh-day Adventist Church Love Feast
(Youth)**

Newly Baptized _____   Date _____

Transfer _____

Male _____   Female _____

Name _____

Address _____

City _____ State _____ Zip _____

Phone Number _____   Birthday _____

Date of baptism _____   Date of transfer _____

Introduced to the church by _____

Hobbies _____

Favorite hymn or gospel song _____

Favorite Bible text/Bible story _____

Which school do you attend? _____ What grade are you? _____

Do you attend Sabbath School? _____ Name your SS teacher _____

Are you interested in working in the church? Yes____ No ____ Perhaps in future ___

If yes, in what area?

    1.   Youth Choir

    2.   Usher Board

    3.   Other

How can the church help you?

Would you like to have a spiritual partner assigned to you?   Yes_____ No _____

Sample 2c: Invitation to Love Feast

The Love Feast Committee Members
cordially invite you to be their guest at
a Love Feast
held in honor of
all recently baptized
and transferred members
on Sabbath July 1, 2000
at Dupont Park
Seventh-day Adventist Church
immediately following the
Divine worship service
in the dining hall

Jonathan Thompson and Lois Miller
Pastor and Minister of Biblical Instruction

R.S.V.P.
Gwendolyn Coleman (301-555-5555)

Sample 2d: The Love Feast Program

Dear Sabbath School member:

Following each quarterly baptism, a *Love Feast* is held to formally welcome our new members into the church family. Two weeks prior to the scheduled *Love Feast,* a representative from the *Love Feast Program* will visit your Sabbath School class and distribute food item requests. We request that you bring your item to the kitchen on the specified day before Sabbath School.

The *Love Feast Program* cannot function without your heart and your hands. Your participation will help make the *Love Feast* a successful endeavor for the entire church family.

Thank you again for your loving participation.

Yours in Christian service,
(Chairperson's Name)
The *Love Feast Program*

Sample 2e: Letter to Board Members

Dear Board Member:

Please bring the following item(s) to the church dining hall before or immediately following Sabbath School on _____,_____.

Item(s):

Thank you,
(Chairperson's Name)
The *Love Feast Program*

Sample 2f: Letter to Sabbath School class members:

Dear Sabbath School class member:

Please bring the items checked below to the church kitchen before the Sabbath School lesson study period on _____.

_____2 Pounds Red Grapes	_____2 Pounds Green Grapes
_____2 Pounds Purple Grapes	_____12 Golden Delicious Apples
_____12 Red Delicious Apples	_____8 Kiwi
_____2 Honeydew Melon	_____2 Cantaloupes
_____2 bags Mixed Dried Fruit	_____12 Peaches
_____12 Oranges	_____12 Nectarines
_____12 Plums	_____1 Large Watermelon
_____3 Pints Strawberries	_____1 Peeled, Cored Pineapple
	(Or 3 cans pineapple chucks)
_____2 8-oz. packages Cream Cheese	_____1 Pound Margarine
_____#10 can Tropical Fruit	_____#10 can Fruit Cocktail
(or 5 15-oz. cans)	(or 5 15-oz. cans)
_____2 Loaves Bread or 2 Doz. Rolls	_____1 Doz. Bananas
_____1 Pound Nuts (Almonds, Pecans,Walnuts, Peanuts)	

Thank you,
(Chairperson's Name)
The *Love Feast Program*
    Note: Adapt this list according to local culture and food availability.

Sample 2g: Program

Opening Prayer and Blessing

Musical Interlude

Love Feast

Introduction of New Members

Presentation of Certificates (photo session)

Right Hand of Fellowship

Musical Selection

Pastoral Remarks

Musical Selection

Closing Prayer

Theme Song "Side By Side" (see *Adventist Youth Sings*).

3. Welcome Wagon

Guidelines for Coordinator

The position of *Welcome Wagon* Coordinator is very important. The coordinator oversees the dinner invitations and coordinates a group meeting for the host families.

Some new members may elect not to accept a position in the church immediately, but they will, for the most part, accept a dinner invitation. By extending dinner invitations to new members, you let them know that they are welcomed and that love does abide in their church home.

The purpose of the invitation is to make new or transferred persons feel that someone cares and to make sure that Sabbath is not a lonely day for new members, but rather a day filled with fellowship.

The purpose of the group meeting is to discuss problems, to share testimonies, and to get committee members to commit to a particular date so that a schedule will be available. This commitment also helps to ensure that each new member receives at least one invitation.

A report must be presented at the *Love Feast Program* meeting, which is usually held once a quarter, depending upon baptisms.

Hospitality is a blessed talent, and your services are very much appreciated. The Lord is happy that you are ministering in this manner.

Sabbath Dinners

Members of the *Welcome Wagon* are requested to periodically invite new members to dine with them on Sabbath. A roster is maintained by the *Welcome Wagon* chairperson to ensure that each new member has been invited to dinner and to provide the proper rotation for host homes *(see sample 3a)*.

Sabbath Dinner with the Pastor

The pastor has a busy schedule which does not always allow him/her to get to know each new member on an individual basis. Therefore, one host family is selected to invite new members, chosen by the chairperson, to get acquainted with the pastor and his/her spouse. This is a time when very special questions can be asked in an informal, yet controlled setting. Because of the nature of this dinner, a home without small children (where interruptions might occur) is preferred. Remember Hebrews 13:2, "Be not forgetful to entertain strangers: for thereby some have entertained angels unawares."

Procedures for the Welcome Wagon Committee

Following are the procedures and methods of the committee:

- Committee will meet as necessary.
- List of new members will be provided quarterly to committee members.
- Leave methods of hosting to individual committee members.
- Provide names of persons who are hosted to the *Welcome Wagon Committee* chairperson.
- Allow a time span of six months to complete the circulation of each current list of new members.
- Extend courtesies to non-member spouse. For example, if non-member spouse answers the telephone, identify yourself, your mission, and extend an invitation.

Sample 3a: Love Feast Committee Welcome Wagon Report

Date _____

6 Hosts/Hostesses	5 participated; 1 did not
Maximum number of invitations extended	8
Minimum number of invitations extended	1
Transfer members invited	1

Welcome Wagon Friends	**Guests**
Coordinator	Ann & John James; Barbara Robb; John Jones
Susan and Robert Black	Mary & Joseph Adams; John Jones; Shirley Smith; Ann & John James; Cathy & William Brown
Amy and James Greene	Katherine Brown
Mary and Marvin Jones	Robert Thomas
Dorothy and Harry Smith	George Bell
	Invited but unable to come: Cathy & William Brown
	Card sent to Addie Carter

4. Nurturing

The Nurturing Committee

The *Nurturing Committee* is a very special part of the *Love Feast Program.* Its members have the closest, most frequent contact with new members. The committee prepares a love package that is presented at the *Love Feast.* This package may consist of the following:

Welcome Letter
Church Directory
Church Support Team List
Appropriate Books
Sunset Calender
Church Manual
Pathfinder brochure
Any other publication felt to be helpful

Remembering Special Days

To make the new person feel remembered and special during his/her first year in the congregation, the *Nurturing Committee* sends a birthday card from the *Love Feast Program*.

Working in the Church

Upon entering a new church, it is important that members—transferred or newly baptized—be placed in areas in which they feel comfortable when ready to work *(see Friendship Sheets 2a and 2b, which list talents and areas of interest)*. Accepting responsibility in the church helps new members feel they belong to the family.

Tours of Church/School Facilities

Tours are available to all new members. Knowing the location of various facilities in the church and school makes for a comfortable transition.

Places to tour include:

Pastor's Study	Dining Area
Church Secretary's Office	Restroom Facilities
Sabbath School Rooms	School Buildings and Facilities
Mothers' Room	

Social Gatherings

The *Love Feast Program* has a *Social Committee* which holds social gatherings during the year. The committee plans wholesome recreation and fellowship activities. It is suggested that this committee include at least two newly baptized members because their input may prove to be most helpful in the committee's planning. It is also suggested that the pastor, assistant pastor, first elder, minister of biblical instruction, and their families be invited to these socials to give the new believers an opportunity to interact with the pastoral staff in a relaxed setting.

Love Feast Program Connection

The *Love Feast Program Connection* members keep in phone contact with new members. These calls are intended to provide fellowship; they are not intended for biblical instruction. Biblical instruction should be left to the Bible instructor or pastor.

Sample 4a: Assignment to Committee Members

To: The *Love Feast Social Committee* Members
From: Darlinda

Subject: Social Committee Report

From all accounts, our social was well received. Due to rainy weather, the number of attendees was less than expected. However, we had more than enough food and the group seemed to enjoy themselves. The social was held on Saturday evening, _____, in the church dining hall from 8:00 p.m. to approximately 10:00 p.m.

The colors for the social were green and white. The menu was:

The committee member assignments were as follows:

Committee Member's Name	*Assignment*
	Fruit Cocktail
	Vegetarian Sloppy Joe
	Potato Chips and Peanuts
	Potato Salad
	Cookies
	Punch/Ginger Ale
	Hamburger Buns and Pickle Chips

Carol Dennis led out in games. We played "Pictionary," "Uno," and other fun games.

The next social is usually scheduled for October. If so, there will be a meeting before the end of August or around the first of September to plan for that social.

Thank you for your help, comments, and suggestions.

Bibliography

Abraham, Ken. *The Disillusioned Christian*. San Bernardino, CA: Here's Life Publishers, 1991.

Anders, Max E. *30 Days to Understanding the Christian Life*. Brentwood, TN: Wolgemuth and Hyatt, 1990.

Annan, Nelson. *More People: Is Church Growth Worth It?* Wheaton: Harold Shaw Publishers, 1987.

Armstrong, Richard Stoll. *The Pastor as Evangelist*. Philadelphia: The Westminster Press, 1984.

Arn, Win, ed. *The Pastor's Church Growth Handbook*. 2 vols. Pasadena: Institute for American Church Growth, 1979.

Arn, Win, and Charles Arn. *The Master's Plan for Making Disciples*. Pasadena: Church Growth Press, 1982.

Augsburger, Myron S. *Matthew*. In Lloyd J. Ogilvie, ed., *The Communicator's Commentary*. Waco: Word, 1982.

Bailey, Keith. *Care of Converts*. Harrisburg: Christian Publications, 1979.

Baker, Delbert, V. Bailey Gillespie, and Alayne Thorpe. *Welcome to the Family*. Takoma Park, MD: Home Study International, 1987.

Barna, George. *The Frog in the Kettle*. Ventura, CA: Regal Books, 1990.

_____. *Marketing the Church. What They Never Taught You About Church Growth*. Colorado Springs: NavPress, 1988.

_____. *User Friendly Churches*. Ventura, CA: Regal Books, 1991.

_____. *What Americans Believe*. Ventura, CA: Regal Books, 1991.

Bellah, Mike. *Baby Boom Believers*. Wheaton, IL: Tyndale House, 1973.

Bruce, F. F. *Paul and His Converts: How Paul Nurtured the Churches He Planted*. Downers Grove, IL: InterVarsity Press, 1985.

Chaney, Charles L., and Ron S. Lewis. *Design for Church Growth*. Nashville: Broadman, 1977.

Cober, Kenneth L. *The Church's Teaching Ministry*. Valley Forge, PA: Judson Press, 1964.

Conn, Harvie M. *Evangelism: Doing Justice and Preaching Grace*. Grand Rapids: Zondervan, 1982.

Cook, Jerry, with Stanley C. Baldwin. *Love, Acceptance and Forgiveness*. Ventura, CA: Regal Books, 1979.

Cress, Sharon M. "Why Members Leave," *PRAXIS*, Summer 1987.

Davis, Anne, and Wade Rowatt, Jr. *Formation for Christian Ministry*. Louisville: Review and Expositor, Southern Baptist Theological Seminary, 1985.

DeVille, Jard. *The Psychology of Witnessing*. Waco: Word, 1980.

Douglas, J. D., ed. *The Work of an Evangelist*. Minneapolis: World Wide Publications, 1984.

Drake, Patricia G. *The Lay Training Committee: What's in it for You?* Washington, DC: The Alban Institute, 1979.

Dudley, Roger L., and Des Cummings, Jr. *Adventures in Church Growth*. Hagerstown, MD: Review and Herald, 1983.

Dunkin, Steve. *Church Advertising: A Practical Guide*. Nashville: Abingdon, 1982.

Edwards, Rex D. *A New Frontier—Every Believer a Minister*. Boise: Pacific Press, 1979.

Engel, James F., and Wilbert Norton. *What's Gone Wrong With the Harvest?* Grand Rapids: Zondervan, 1975.

Fowler, John W. "Caring for New Converts," *Ministry,* April 1979.

Frederikson, Roger L. *John* in Lloyd Ogilvie, ed. *The Communicator's Commentary.* Waco: Word, 1985.

Fryling, Alice. *Disciplemaker's Handbook.* Downer's Grove, IL: InterVarsity Press, 1989.

Gallup, George, Jr., and David Poling. *The Search for America's Faith.* Nashville: Abingdon, 1980.

Gallup, George, Jr., and George O'Connell. *Who Do Americans Say That I Am?* Philadelphia: Westminster Press, 1986.

George, Carl. *Empty Pews, Empty Streets.* Columbia, MD: Columbia Union Conference of Seventh-day Adventists, 1988.

Gibbs, Eddie. *I Believe in Church Growth.* Grand Rapids: Eerdmans, 1981.

Graham, Billy. *A Biblical Standard for Evangelists.* Minneapolis: World Wide Publications, 1984.

Green, Michael. *Evangelism in the Early Church.* Grand Rapids: Eerdmans, 1970.

_____. *Evangelism Through The Local Church.* Nashville: Oliver Nelson, 1992.

_____. *Freed to Serve: Training and Equipping for Ministry.* Dallas: Word, 1983.

_____. *To Corinth with Love.* Waco: Word, 1988.

Griffin, E. M. *Making Friends and Making Them Count.* Downers Grove, IL: InterVarsity Press, 1987.

Hadaway, C. Kirk. *What Can We Do About Church Dropouts?* Nashville: Abingdon, 1990.

Hadidian, Allen. *Discipleship: Helping Other Christians Grow.* Chicago: Moody Press, 1987.

Harper, Michael. *Let My People Grow.* Plainfield, NJ: Logos International, 1977.

Henrichsen, Walter A. *Disciples are Made—Not Born.* Wheaton, IL: Victor Books, 1986.

Hinson, E. Glenn. *The Church: Design for Survival.* Nashville: Broadman, 1967.

Houck, Fannie L. *Beyond Baptism.* Hagerstown, MD: Review and Herald, 1987.

Hull, Bill. *Jesus Christ Disciple Maker.* Old Tappan, NJ: Fleming H. Revell Co., 1978.

Hunter, George G., III. *The Contagious Congregation: Frontiers in Evangelism and Church Growth.* Nashville: Abingdon, 1979.

Hunter, Kent R. *Foundations for Church Growth.* New Haven, MO: Leader Publishing Co., 1973.

_____. *Reaping and Keeping the Harvest.* Corunna, IN: Church Growth Center, 1982.

Huston, Sterling W. *Crusade Evangelism and the Local Church.* Minneapolis: World Wide Publications, 1986.

Jewett, Dick. *Orientation for New Adventists.* Hagerstown, MD: Review and Herald, 1978.

Johnson, Ben Campbell. *Rethinking Evangelism.* Philadelphia: Westminster Press, 1987.

Johnson, Bruce. "A Myth Is as Good as a Mile: All New Converts Soon Leave," *North Pacific Union Gleaner,* November 6, 1989.

Johnson, Douglas W. *The Care and Feeding of Volunteers.* Nashville: Abingdon, 1978.

Johnsson, William G. "The Missing Tell Us Why," *Adventist Review,* September 7, 1989.

Kroll, Woodrow. *10 First Steps for the New Christian.* Lincoln, NE: The Good News Broadcasting Association, Inc., 1992.

Land, Gary, ed. *Adventism in America.* Grand Rapids: Eerdmans, 1986.

Lewis, Jo H., and Gordon A. Palmer. *What Every Christian Should Know.* Wheaton, IL: Victor Books, 1989.

Lindgren, Alvin J., and Norman Shawchuck. *Let My People Go: Empowering Laity for Ministry.* Nashville: Abingdon, 1980.

Martin, Linford Lee. *The Challenge of the Empty Pew.* Manhasset, NY: Greater New York Conference of Seventh-day Adventists, 1992.

Martin, William. *A Prophet With Honor.* New York: William Morrow and Company, 1991.

McGavran, Donald A. *Back to Basics in Church Growth.* Wheaton, IL: Tyndale House, 1984.

_____. *Understanding Church Growth.* Grand Rapids: Eerdmans, 1980.

McGavran, Donald A., and Winfield C. Arn, *Ten Steps for Church Growth*. New York: Harper and Row, 1977.

McGavran, Donald A., and George G. Hunter, III. *Church Growth: Strategies That Work*. Nashville, Abingdon, 1980.

McIntosh, Gary, and Glen Martin. *Finding Them, Keeping Them: Effective Strategies for Evangelism and Assimilation in the Local Church*. Nashville: Broadman Press, 1992.

Miller, Herb. *Evangelism's Open Secrets*. St. Louis: CBP Press, 1977.

———. *How to Build a Magnetic Church*. Nashville: Abingdon, 1987.

Moeller, John R., Director, *1990 Cobb County, Georgia, Data Report*. Marietta, GA: Cobb County Department of Planning & Zoning, 1990.

Neuhaus, Richard John. *Freedom for Ministry*. San Francisco: Harper and Row, 1979.

Peters, George W. *A Theology of Church Growth*. Grand Rapids: Zondervan, 1981.

Ratz, Calvin, Frank Tillapaugh, and Myron Augsburger. *Mastering Outreach and Evangelism*. Portland: Multnomah Press, 1990.

Savage, John S. *The Apathetic and Bored Church Member*. Reynoldsburg, OH: LEAD Consultants, Inc., 1976.

Schaller, Lyle E. *Activating the Passive Church*. Nashville: Abingdon, 1981.

———. *Assimilating New Members*. Nashville: Abingdon, 1978.

———. "Denominational or Independent? Where Are the Advantages?" *The Clergy Journal*.

———. *44 Ways To Increase Church Attendance*. Nashville: Abingdon, 1988.

Smith, Bailey E. *Real Evangelism*. Nashville: Broadman, 1978.

Stebbins, Tom. *Evangelism by the Book*. Camp Hill, PA: Christian Publications, 1991.

Stevens, R. Paul. *Liberating the Laity*. Downers Grove, IL: InterVarsity Press, 1985.

Stott, John R. W. *Christian Mission in the Modern World*. Downers Grove, IL: InterVarsity Press, 1975.

Stutzman, Ervin R. *Welcome! A Biblical and Practical Guide to Receiving New Members*. Scottdale, PA: Herald Press, 1990.

Sweazey, George E. *The Church as Evangelist*. San Francisco: Harper and Row, 1978.

Sweazy, Carl M. *Evangelism That Evangelizes!* Ventura, CA: Clark's Printing Co., 1968.

Thomas G. Ernest. *Twenty-five Ways to Assimilate New Members*. Nashville: Tidings, 1973.

Thompson, W. Oscar, Jr. *Concentric Circles of Concern*. Nashville: Broadman, 1981.

Tillapaugh, Frank R. *Unleashing the Church*. Ventura, CA: Regal Books, 1982.

Tuttle, Robert G., Jr. *Someone Out There Needs Me*. Grand Rapids: Zondervan, 1983.

Wagner, C. Peter, *Church Growth and the Whole Gospel*. San Francisco: Harper and Row, 1981.

———. *Leading Your Church to Growth*. Ventura, CA: Regal Books, 1884.

———. *Strategies for Church Growth*. Ventura, CA: Regal Books, 1987.

———. *Your Church Can Be Healthy*. Nashville: Abingdon, 1979.

———. *Your Church Can Grow*. Ventura, CA: Regal Books, 1984.

Wagner, C. Peter, with Win Arn and Elmer Towns. *Church Growth: The State of the Art*. Wheaton, IL: Tyndale House, 1986.

Warren, Rick. *The Purpose Driven Church*. Grand Rapids: Zondervan, 1995.

Watson, David. *Called and Committed: World-Changing Discipleship*. Wheaton, IL: Harold Shaw Publishers, 1982.

White, Ellen G. *Christ's Object Lessons*. Washington, DC: Review and Herald, 1941.

———. *Evangelism*. Washington, DC: Review and Herald, 1970.

Widmer, Myron. "My Friends, the Missing," *Adventist Review*, May 4, 1989.

Wilson, Carl. *With Christ in the School of Disciple Making*. Grand Rapids: Zondervan, 1976.

Wirt, Sherwood Eliot. *Evangelism: The Next Ten Years*. Waco: Word, 1978.

Wood, David. *A Shepherd's Guide to Caring and Keeping*. Pasadena: Church Growth, 1986.